Guide to Criminal Law for Texas

Second Edition

Barbara A. Belbot
University of Houston-Downtown

Australia • Canada • Mexico • Singapore • Spain • United Kingdom • United States

COPYRIGHT © 2002 Wadsworth Group. Wadsworth, is an imprint of the Wadsworth Group, a division of Thomson Learning, Inc. Thomson Learning™ is a trademark used herein under license.

ALL RIGHTS RESERVED. No part of this work covered by the copyright hereon may be reproduced or used in any form or by any means—graphic, electronic, or mechanical, including photocopying, recording, taping, Web distribution, or information storage and retrieval systems—without the prior written permission of the publisher.

Printed in the United States of America

1 2 3 4 5 6 7 04 03 02 01 00

For permission to use material from this text, contact us by **Web**: http://www.thomsonrights.com
Fax: 1-800-730-2215 **Phone**: 1-800-730-2214

For more information, contact
Wadsworth/Thomson Learning
10 Davis Drive
Belmont, CA 94002-3098
USA

For more information about our products, contact us:
Thomson Learning Academic Resource Center
1-800-423-0563
http://www.wadsworth.com

International Headquarters
Thomson Learning
International Division
290 Harbor Drive, 2nd Floor
Stamford, CT 06902-7477
USA

UK/Europe/Middle East/South Africa
Thomson Learning
Berkshire House
168-173 High Holborn
London WC1V 7AA
United Kingdom

Asia
Thomson Learning
60 Albert Complex, #15-01
Singapore 189969

Canada
Nelson Thomson Learning
1120 Birchmount Road
Toronto, Ontario M1K 5G4
Canada

ISBN 0-534-56365-1

CONTENTS

CHAPTER ONE – THE NATURE, ORIGINS, AND PURPOSES OF CRIMINAL LAW	
Introduction	1
Some Important General Code Provisions	1
Locating Texas Criminal Law	3
Classifying Crimes	7
Final Comments	11
Multiple Choice Questions	11
CHAPTER TWO – CONSTITUTIONAL LIMITS ON CRIMINAL LAW	
Introduction	15
The Ex Post Facto Clause	15
The Equal Protection Clause	18
Void-for-Vagueness and Freedom of Speech	20
Void-for-Vagueness and Due Process	21
Final Comments	23
Multiple Choice Questions	23
CHAPTER THREE - THE GENERAL PRINCIPLES OF CRIMINAL LIABILITY: THE REQUIREMENT OF ACTION	
Introduction	26
Final Comments	32
Multiple Choice Questions	32
CHAPTER FOUR – THE GENERAL PRINCIPLES OF CRIMINAL LIABILITY: MENS REA, CONCURRENCE, CAUSATION	
Introduction	36
Culpable Mental State	36
The Causation Requirement	39
Strict Liability	41
Final Comments	41
Multiple Choice Questions	42
CHAPTER FIVE – PARTIES TO CRIME: COMPLICITY AND VICARIOUS LIABILITY	
Introduction	44
Complicity Statutes	44
Final Comments	52
Multiple Choice Questions	52
CHAPTER SIX – UNCOMPLETED CRIMES: ATTEMPT, CONSPIRACY, AND SOLICITATION	
Introduction	55
Attempting to Commit a Crime	55
Conspiring to Commit a Crime	62
Criminal Solicitation	68
Final Comments	69
Multiple Choice Questions	69
CHAPTER SEVEN – DEFENSES TO CRIMINAL LIABILITY: JUSTIFICATIONS	
Introduction	72
Self Defense	72
Defense of Property	80
Sanctioned Uses of Force	83
The Necessity or Choice of Evils Defense	83
Final Thoughts	84
Multiple Choice Questions	85

CHAPTER EIGHT – DEFENSES TO CRIMINAL LIABILITY: EXCUSES	
Introduction	88
The Insanity Defense	88
Mistake of Fact	92
Mistake of Law	93
Intoxication	93
Duress	94
Entrapment	95
Age	96
Final Comments	97
Multiple Choice Questions	98
CHAPTER NINE – CRIMES AGAINST PERSONS: HOMICIDE	
Introduction	100
The Murder Statute	100
Capital Punishment: Texas Style	103
Final Comments	109
Multiple Choice Questions	109
CHAPTER TEN – CRIMES AGAINST PERSONS: CRIMINAL SEXUAL CONDUCT AND OTHERS	
Introduction	112
Sexual Assault	112
Assault	120
Final Comments	123
Multiple Choice Questions	123
CHAPTER ELEVEN – CRIMES AGAINST HABITATION: BURGLARY AND ARSON	
Introduction	126
Burglary	126
Criminal Trespass	130
Arson	130
Criminal Mischief	131
Final Comments	132
Multiple Choice Questions	132
CHAPTER TWELVE – CRIMES AGAINST PROPERTY	
Introduction	135
Theft	135
Fraud	140
Robbery	141
Final Comments	143
Multiple Choice Questions	143
CHAPTER THIRTEEN – CRIMES AGAINST PUBLIC ORDER AND MORALS	
Introduction	146
Disorderly Conduct	146
Rioting, Obstructing, and Disturbing	148
Other Public Order Offenses	150
Final Comments	150
Multiple Choice Questions	150
ANSWER KEY	153

CHAPTER ONE

THE NATURE, ORIGINS, AND PURPOSES OF CRIMINAL LAW

INTRODUCTION

This chapter introduces you to the Texas Penal Code, how it classifies criminal offenses and provides for their punishment, specifically:

(1) some of the more important general provisions of the Code,
(2) how the criminal law of Texas can be located and how cases interpreting the law can be accessed,
(3) the Code's scheme for classifying offenses,
(4) the Code's punishment philosophy and provisions for punishment.

You will learn better and understand more if you follow along with the discussion in this chapter and throughout the supplement by consulting the relevant provisions of the Texas Penal Code (referred throughout as the T.P.C.). This supplement will describe and quote portions of the T.P.C., but there is no substitute for actually reading the code. Sometimes code provisions get convoluted enough to warrant a reading out loud. Only by working through and finding provisions of the statute on your own, will you appreciate the complexities, frustrations, and fun (yes, fun) of the law. Purchase a Texas Penal Code and begin a journey into the creative, ever-changing study of the criminal law as defined and enforced in the Lone Star State!

SOME IMPORTANT GENERAL CODE PROVISIONS

Texas is one of 25 states that have abolished common law crimes and is considered a code jurisdiction. According to section 1.03 of the Texas Penal Code (T.P.C.), conduct is not an offense unless it is so defined by statute or other legislative act. Section 1.03 establishes two important notions:

(1) the codified penal code supersedes all common-law offenses and,
(2) the "legality" principle - there can be no crime without a law

The T.P.C. was first enacted in 1856, and was revised for the first time in 1974. The 1974 revised code is the penal code still in use although it has been significantly amended over the last two decades to include new offenses, changed definitions, and different punishment schemes. It retains, however, the organization and structure of the 1974 revisions. Although the 1974 revisions were substantial, they did not radically change the criminal law in the state of

Texas. The revised code introduced greater clarity, simplicity and order to the law. The T.P.C. does not include all Texas penal law. There are provisions scattered throughout the civil statutes that impose criminal fines and punishment, most of which involve regulatory type offenses. For example, section 195.004 of the Texas Health and Safety Code makes it a Class C misdemeanor to fail, neglect, or refuse to fill out a birth or death certificate. Section 13.007 of the Texas Election Code makes it a Class B misdemeanor to make false statements on an application to vote. Juveniles who engage in unlawful conduct are adjudicated under the provisions of the Texas Family Code. The Penal Code makes clear in section 1.03, however, that any state penal statute, municipal ordinance, or administrative rule or regulation is of no effect to the extent it overlaps, duplicates, or conflicts with a T.P.C. provision.

Jurisdiction

Section 1.04 of the T.P.C. establishes that Texas has jurisdiction over:

(1) offenses any element of which occur in the state;
(2) out-of-state attempts to commit offenses within the state;
(3) out-of-state conspiracies, if an act in furtherance of the conspiracy occurs inside the state;
(4) any offense under the law of another state that is also an offense in Texas, if any conduct including attempt, solicitation, conspiracy or other conduct that establishes criminal responsibility for its commission occurs in Texas;
(5) any offense based on an omission to perform a duty imposed on an actor by state law regardless of the location of the actor at the time of the offense;
(6) if the offense is criminal homicide and the body of the victim is found in Texas, it is presumed that the victim's death occurred in Texas.

Purpose of the Criminal Law

The Texas legislature states in section 1.02 that the general purpose of the criminal law is to deal with conduct that causes harm to individuals or public interests the state should be protecting, however, criminal responsibility should attach only to conduct that is unjustifiable or inexcusable, that is, guilty conduct. In the language of the statute is seen the age-old controversy surrounding criminal law. Should the law emphasize a subjective theory of criminal liability and focus on the offender's moral guilt or should it focus on the harm done to the victim and the offender's objective manifestation of criminality?

The legislature states that the code is intended to achieve certain objectives, including deterring the public from committing crime, deterring the convicted offender from committing further crimes, and rehabilitating offenders. The legislature also states that the law is designed to provide for penalties that are proportionate to the seriousness of the offense and that recognize that individual offenders have different potential for rehabilitation. No where in section 1.02 is retribution listed as an objective of the Texas Penal Code.

Definitions

Forty-eight key terms found throughout the Penal Code are defined in section 1.07. The definitions are applied whenever that particular term is used in the Code. The definition section is crucial to understanding the meaning of different criminal offenses. Take for instance the term "person." If an offense proscribes certain behavior by a person, section 1.07 tells us that a person may include individuals <u>and</u> corporations and associations. On the other hand, if the code proscribes conduct by an individual, the offense can be committed only by "a human being who has been born and is alive." The term "deadly weapon" includes "anything manifestly designed, made, or adapted for the purpose of inflicting death or serious bodily injury, and "anything that in the manner of its use or intended use is capable of causing death or serious bodily injury." Chairs, baseball bats, vases, bottles, sling shots – the list of deadly weapons is endless! Section 1.07 does not include definitions of all the important terms found in the code. Some are defined in the specific section of the code where they are used.

Legislative Changes

The Texas legislature meets every two years, and, among many other things, it debates and passes amendments to the Penal Code. There are proposals every legislative session for the enactment of new criminal offenses, changes in the scope and definitions of offenses already on the books, and changes in the classification of specific offenses or their punishment. It is important to remember that the Penal Code will change every two years. Sometimes the changes are numerous. Sometimes they are a dramatic departure from the past. Sometimes the changes provide better organization and structure the code to make it easier to use. New criminal offenses reflect changes in society. When computers became a part of our daily personal and commercial lives, it was necessary to create statutes that addressed crimes that could only be committed with or because of computer technology, such as section 33.02 of the T.P.C. that defines the crime of breaching computer security. On the other hand, stalking statutes were enacted during the past ten years to deal with behavior that was not new. Stalking laws resulted from a change of attitude that reflected a greater sensitivity and understanding toward victims of stalking behavior, and recognized that stalkers often turn dangerous.

Exercises:
What new criminal laws were passed by the Texas legislature during its most recent session? What proposed criminal laws were not passed? If the legislature is meeting currently, what changes to the Penal Code are being proposed? Who are the legislators proposing the laws and the public interest groups supporting them? If it is a legislative year, collect news articles about the new proposals.

It is easy to follow the Texas legislature by accessing the Texas Legislature Online at http://www.capitol.tx.us/. You can read legislation that has been proposed and follow it through legislative hearings, amendments, and votes. You can easily limit your search to criminal justice related bills. You can also locate the entire set of Texas statutes online at http://www.capitol.state.tx.us/statutes/statutes.html.

LOCATING TEXAS CRIMINAL LAW

How the Penal Code is Organized

As already mentioned, with the exception of certain regulatory offenses, the criminal law is found in the Texas Penal Code. Each separate offense is assigned a section number. Section numbers are also assigned to other important criminal law concepts such as self-defense, the insanity defense, and criminal responsibility for the conduct of another. If you know the section of the code that addresses the offense or concept you want to look at, turn to that section of the code. For instance, if you know that aggravated robbery is defined in section 29.03, turn to that section. Since there are many versions of the Penal Code available, each with their own format and pagination, offenses are located by section number. Code sections are arranged numerically, starting with section 1.01 through section 71.05.

The sections are also arranged into chapters. Each chapter includes those sections of the code that address a particular type of offense. When a new crime is enacted, it is placed in the chapter that best describes the nature of the offense and is given a section number that is not currently assigned to a crime already in the chapter. For example, Chapter 19 includes all the sections of the T.P.C. that deal with criminal homicide. The scheme is sometimes less than perfect, however. Chapter 22 includes all the sections that deal with the crime of assault: assault, sexual assault, aggravated assault, aggravated sexual assault, and injury to a child, elderly individual, or disabled individual. Chapter 22 also includes crimes that are less obviously assault-like: abandoning or endangering a child, deadly conduct, terrorist threat, aiding suicide, tampering with a consumer product, and leaving a child in a vehicle.

If you do not know the section number of an offense or the chapter in which it is located, look at the topic index in the back of the version of the code you are using. Use it like any other topic index, look for key words and a section number will be provided. If the key word you chose is not listed, brainstorm and look for other key words.

If the offense you are looking for was enacted after the version of your Penal Code was published, you will not find it! Seek out the most recent Penal Code! The law changes every two years. Even if the offense is listed in your older version, **be careful**. There may have been changes to the definition of that offense during the last legislative session. You may be referring to old law.

Do not forget to refer to section 1.07 to define important terms in the offense you are researching. Statutes are written in legalese, which is a stilted, formal language. Read the statutes carefully and understand that **every** word in the statute has been placed there for a reason. Be mindful of words like "and," "or," "either," "including but not limited to."

Vernon's Texas Code Annotated

Every state has an official publication of its statutes. In Texas, the official publication of the criminal law is found in Vernon's Texas Code Annotated, a set of three volumes labeled "Penal Code," which is a part of a large multi-volume set that includes all the state's laws. Vernon's is an especially useful place to research the criminal law because in addition to the text of the laws, there are annotations following the text that include extremely helpful information. The text of each section of the Penal Code is followed by notes about the legislative history of the section, when the section was passed and when and what amendments have been made to the section. The annotations also include a listing of law review articles and legal treatises about the particular section. Most importantly, under the heading "Notes of Decisions" the annotations include brief descriptions of cases decided by courts who have interpreted the section, the names of the cases, and where they can be located (citations). For lawyers and other scholars of the law, reading the text of the law is only the beginning of understanding what the law means. The next step is to read case opinions that have interpreted the law. Vernon's is one way to locate the names and citations of those cases.

There are often long lists of cases interpreting the various provisions of a section of the Penal Code. Of course, the more important or controversial the section, more cases will be listed. In Texas, the state district courts are the trial courts that sit over the trial of criminal felony cases. Judges in the state district courts do not issue written opinions about their rulings. If a criminal case is appealed to the Texas Court of Appeals, however, the intermediate court of appeals that heard the appeal will often write an opinion. Many of those written opinions are published. Published opinions have citations that designate where in the law books the opinions can be found. If the decision of the Texas Court of Appeals is appealed to the Texas Court of Criminal Appeals, an opinion will usually be written and published. Vernon's Penal Code is one way for researchers to find the opinions of the intermediate Texas Courts of Appeal and the Texas Court of Criminal Appeals. Brief abstracts describe a bit about what the case decided so the researcher can determine whether the case is worth reading.

A Note About Court Opinions

Not all court opinions carry equal weight in terms of precedential value. The court of last resort in Texas for criminal matters is the Texas Court of Criminal Appeals. The decisions of that court are the final say. The Court of Criminal Appeals has jurisdiction over the entire state. Once that court has spoken about a particular matter, every court in the state must follow its interpretation of the law.

The Texas Court of Appeals is really composed of 14 different appeals courts that serve different parts of the state. Each Court of Appeals has jurisdiction in a specific geographical region of the state. Their decisions are precedent only for the state district and county courts located within their jurisdiction. When using the Vernon's statutes, the researcher will obviously pay close attention to the opinions rendered by the Texas Court of Criminal Appeals. The researcher will also look for the cases decided most recently. If the Texas Court of Criminal Appeals has not rendered an opinion about a particular provision of the code, the researcher will look to opinions rendered by the Texas Court of Appeals. He or she will first look for opinions rendered by the appeals court that includes the jurisdiction where the case is located. If that Court of Appeals has not rendered a decision on the matter at issue, the researcher looks to the other intermediate courts of appeal to see if they have entertained the issue.

Because hard cover law books are extremely expensive, every year publishers put together all the recent changes in the law in a paperback version to update the most current hard cover volume. The yearly update is called a pocket part because it literally slips into a pocket placed in the back cover of the hardbound volume that it updates. The pocket not only updates the statute, it also contains the abstracts, names, and citations of court opinions that have been rendered since the hardbound volume was printed. It is essential to check the pocket parts in order to find the most recent law and court cases.

Other Ways to Find Relevant Cases

There are other ways to find court opinions about Texas criminal law. One important research tool is the Texas Digest. The Digest is a comprehensive listing of cases that have interpreted all the provisions of the Texas statutes. By looking under those volumes in the Digest for criminal law, you will find cases that interpret the Code's various provisions. The Digest is also updated each year with pocket parts that list the cases decided since the hardbound volume was published. In the front of the Digest's volumes that pertain to the criminal law, you will find an outline of topics. Next to each topic is a symbol in the shape of a key and a number. The number is called the key number. Find the topic you want to research and note its key number. Turn to the key number in the criminal law volumes to find an exhaustive listing of cases interpreting that topic.

If you are lucky enough to have access to a computer database of court cases, your research will be considerably facilitated. There are two commercial electronic (WESTLAW and LEXIS) databases that allow research to be conducted using key words and phrases. The electronic databases are very expensive to use and access is typically limited to persons who are affiliated with the firm or academic institution that has purchased access to the data.

There is an Internet site accessible to the public that publishes **some** decisions by Texas courts. To find out what cases are available, go to the site for The Texas Judiciary at http://www.courts.state.tx.us/. This site provides lots of information about the Texas court system as well as recent opinions written by the Texas Supreme Court, the Texas Court of Criminal Appeals, and the Texas Court of Appeals. At this time, only opinions written over the past two to three years are reported over the Internet. Cases are being added, and the site will become more useful over time. The Texas Judiciary site is only helpful if you know the name of the parties involved in the case or the date the case was decided. There are no research tools or topic indexes to assist you in locating a relevant case about a particular legal question. The Internet site for the National Center for State Courts at http://www.ncsc.dni.us/ provides links to all the state court web pages. You can visit the web page for the state of your choice to determine what court opinions are available for that state over the Internet.

Locating an Actual Case

Once you have the name and citation of a case that sounds like it deals with the issue you are interested in, the next step is to find the case and read it. Opinions issued by the Texas Courts of Appeal and the Texas Court of Criminal Appeals are found in the South Western Reporters, a multi-volume set of published court cases, both civil and criminal. The South Western Reporter is published by West Publishing Company and is a unit of West's national reporter system. Texas criminal cases decided between 1892 - 1931 are found in the set called South Western Reporters. Criminal cases decided between 1932 - to the current date are found in the set called South Western Reporters 2d. Volumes are numbered, beginning with number one. As new cases are published, new volumes are added and the numbers increase.

Case citations are easy to understand. After the name of a case, there is a string of numbers. That string is known as the case citation. For example, State of Texas v. Johnnie BadGuy, 690 S.W.2d 789 translates into:

    Case name – State of Texas v. Johnnie BadGuy
    Case Citation – volume 690 of the South Western Reporters 2d, page 789

There will be other information following the citation in parentheses, such as (Tex. App. – El Paso 1995). The parentheses tell us that this case was decided in 1995 by the Texas Court of Appeals located in El Paso. You may see something like (Tex. Crim. App. 1988) which tells us that this case was decided by the Texas Court of Criminal Appeals in 1988. Case citations often include other information about the history of the case as it was appealed through the Texas court system, but that information is not important for us to master here.

> **Exercises:**
> Find the Texas Annotated Penal Code and look up section 9.31 concerning self-defense. Read the statute. Find a case citation in the "Notes of Decisions" that addresses the retreat doctrine. How does the note describe the case, what court decided the case, and when was it decided? Now find the case in the South Western Reporters 2d. Read the entire case and summarize it in two paragraphs.
> Congratulations!
>
> Look at Chapter 48 of the Penal Code. Read sections 48.01 and 48.02. Do you agree that the behavior those statutes criminalizes should be against the law? Defend your reasons.

CLASSIFYING CRIMES

Every state classifies its crimes into more and less serious offenses. How a crime is classified determines the type and length of punishment. The more serious offenses that involve spending time in the Big House for a year or longer are felonies. The less serious crimes that involve incarceration in the county jail for less than one year or no incarceration, just a fine are misdemeanors. Beyond that common distinction, the states differ considerably in their classification schemes.

Once convicted of a specific crime, the offender's punishment must be within the parameters defined by the Penal Code. Judges and juries do not have the discretion to go outside the law and devise punishments that are not provided for in the criminal laws. Texas is unique in that the law allows the jury that convicted the offender to decide how the offender should be punished. Many states allow only the judge who presided at the trial to decide punishment. According to the Texas Code of Criminal Procedure, it is the offender's choice as to whether punishment is assessed by the judge or the jury, with the exception of capital felony cases when the State seeks the death penalty. In cases where the death penalty is sought, the jury that convicted the offender must participate in the sentencing process.

> **Exercises:**
> Read Chapters 22 and 29 of the Penal Code and notice how the different but similar offenses within those two Chapters have been given different classifications by the state legislature.

Punishment Provisions

The type and length of punishment for each offense depends on the classification ascribed to the offense. Once you know a crime's classification you know the punishment facing an offender convicted of that crime. Toward the end of each section that defines a criminal

7

offense, there is a subsection that defines how that particular crime is classified. Chapter 12 of the Texas Penal Code lays out how the various levels of misdemeanors and felonies are sanctioned.

Misdemeanors

Class A misdemeanors are the most serious of this level of offense and are punished by a fine not to exceed $4000.00, confinement in jail for a term not to exceed one year, or both the fine and the confinement. Notice that the statute provides for a range of punishment. The judge or jury need not impose the entire $4000 fine. No fine has to be imposed at all. A jail term of up to one year is available, but an entire year need not be imposed. The range gives the judge or juries the ability to exercise a certain amount of discretion in the sentencing decision, allowing them to consider the circumstances of the case before them.

Class B misdemeanors can lead to a fine of up to $2000.00 and jail time not to exceed 180 days. By jail time, the statute means incarceration in the county jail facility as opposed to the state's correctional institutions. The least serious Class C misdemeanor can be sanctioned only by a fine not to exceed $500.00.

Felonies

The most serious felony is a capital felony. There is only one capital felony offense and that is for certain kinds of homicide as defined in Chapter 19 of the T.P.C. If the State seeks the death penalty for a capital murder, the convicted offender must be punished either by death or life in prison. If the State does not seek the death penalty for a capital murder the only punishment available is life imprisonment. The State is not required by law to seek death for a capital murder.

First-degree felony: imprisonment for life or for any term not more than 99 years or less than five years. A fine not to exceed $10,000.00.

Second-degree felony: imprisonment for a term of not more than 20 years or less than two years. A fine not to exceed $10,000.00.

Third-degree felony: imprisonment for a term of not more than 10 years or less than two years. A fine not to exceed $10,000.00.

Imprisonment for first, second, and third-degree felonies takes place in the Texas Department of Criminal Justice - Institutional Division. Convicted offenders are sent to whatever state correctional facility suits their particular prisoner classification and the needs of the agency.

State jail felony: confinement in a state jail for a term of not more than two years or less than 180 days. A fine not to exceed $10,000.00.

State jail felonies were created by the Texas legislature in 1993, amid much controversy as part of the most sweeping sentencing reform legislation in the history of the state. The legislature made many non-violent property and drug offenses state jail felonies. It also doubled the time to be served by most violent offenders by limiting the amount of good time credits they could earn. The rationale for the reform was to balance the need to "get tough on crime" with the need to "get smart on crime." Getting tough involved increasing convictions, the number of offenders in prison and the length of time offenders stay incarcerated. "Getting smart on crime" involved finding less expensive alternatives than the traditional prison to protect the public safety.

Beginning on September 1, 1994, numerous offenses in the Penal Code were assigned to a punishment range called the state jail felony, sometimes referred to as a fourth-degree felony. A state jail felon serves time in a state jail felony facility without the opportunity to acquire good time credits. The most significant aspect of the state jail felony sentence is that after a judge or jury assesses such a punishment, the judge must suspend the sentence and place the defendant on community supervision. As a condition of this mandatory community supervision, the judge also may order the defendant to serve short periods of time in a county jail or a state jail. The judge may also confine a state jail felon to a community restitution center, a substance abuse treatment center, or a local boot camp. If the defendant has previously been convicted of a felony, the judge is not required to suspend the sentence and place him or her on community supervision. If a defendant on community supervision for a state jail felony violates a condition of that supervision, the judge may revoke the supervision and order the defendant to serve time in the state jail facility.

State jail felonies largely include previous third-degree felonies that involved low level property offenders. Examples of state jail felonies include theft of property valued at $1500.00 or more but less than $20,000.00 and unauthorized use of a vehicle. A few state jail felonies were formerly first and second-degree felonies: burglary of a building, possession or delivery of less than one gram of a penalty 1 controlled substance. Other state jail felonies were formerly misdemeanors: criminally negligent homicide, criminal nonsupport, injury to a child, elderly person or a disabled person by criminal negligence.

State jail felony facilities are different than the state correctional institutions where convicted felons are sent. State jails are also not the same as the county jails that house convicted misdemeanants and pretrial detainees. State jails are unique institutions that are part of the state's correctional apparatus and were created at the same time the legislature created the state jail felony classification. The idea is that the state jail division of the Texas Department of Criminal Justice works in conjunction with community justice agencies to develop and adopt work, rehabilitation, education, and recreation programs within the state jails.

A state jail felony becomes a third-degree felony if it is shown at trial that the offender used or exhibited a deadly weapon during the commission of the offense or while fleeing from the crime. If the offender who is convicted of a state jail felony has been previously convicted of murder, capital murder, indecency with a child, aggravated kidnapping, aggravated sexual assault, or aggravated robbery, his or her state jail felony conviction is automatically enhanced to a third-degree felony.

Repeat and Habitual Offenders

From a convicted felon's perspective, perhaps the most important part of Chapter 12 addresses penalties for repeat and habitual offenders. Continuing to commit and be convicted of crimes has serious consequences. The argument against habitual offender statutes is that offenders are punished more than once for their crimes: the first time when they are convicted and serve their sentence and a second time when the punishment for a new and different conviction is enhanced because they are repeat offenders. An argument in favor of habitual offender statutes is that repeat offenders obviously did not learn their lesson the first time and need the threat of enhanced punishment. Secondly, repeat offenders are a greater threat to society and deserve enhanced punishment. The courts have upheld the constitutionality of habitual offender statutes.

The Texas Penal Code provides that punishment for a second-degree felony conviction shall be enhanced to punishment for a first-degree felony conviction if it is shown that the offender has been convicted once before of a prior felony. This means that instead of facing a sentence of 2 to 20 years in prison, the convicted habitual offender faces imprisonment of between 5 and 99 years. If it is shown that the convicted offender of a first-degree felony has been once before convicted of a prior felony, his or her punishment shall be enhanced to any term of not more than 99 years or less than 15 years. Instead of facing 5 to 99 years, he or she faces 15 to 99 years.

During the "get tough on crime" era of the last decade, legislators have responded to the public's concerns by making the habitual offender statutes even tougher, especially for repeat sex offenders. In 1994, the 74th Texas Legislature mandated automatic life sentences for persons convicted of:

- aggravated sexual assault,
- aggravated kidnapping with the intent to violate or abuse the victim sexually,
- burglary with the intent to commit a sex offense or indecency with a child

and

IF the defendant had been previously convicted of two felony offenses at least one of which was for:
- indecency with a child,
- sexual assault,
- aggravated sexual assault,
- prohibited sexual conduct,
- sexual performance by a child,
- possession of or promotion of child pornography,
- aggravated kidnapping with the intent to violate or abuse the victim sexually,
- or burglary with the intent to commit a sex offense.

Not only can the punishment for third, second, and first-degree felonies be enhanced, penalties for repeat misdemeanors can be enhanced as well. Offenders who repeat state jail felonies can also find themselves facing more serious sanctions: third and, in certain circumstances, second-degree felonies.

Interestingly, a life sentence in Texas does not mean that the convicted offender will never see the "freeworld" again. Texas does not have a life without parole sentence. A prisoner who is serving a life sentence for a capital felony must serve at least 40 calendar years without consideration of good conduct time. If he or she is a habitual offender and is serving an automatic life sentence for one of the crimes described above, they must stay in prison for at least 35 calendar years without consideration of good conduct time.

The Penal Code does not address the availability of community supervision as an alternative punishment to incarceration. Article 42 of the Texas Code of Criminal Procedure describes under what circumstances a judge can suspend a sentence of incarceration and place a convicted offender on community supervision. Article 42 also provides for the award of good time credit to inmates who are incarcerated. Good time credits can significantly reduce how much of a sentence the offender actually serves. Finally, Article 42 describes the parole eligibility process. In order to appreciate fully the sentencing scheme in Texas, you have to link together the various provisions of the Penal Code and the Code of Criminal Procedure.

> **Exercises:**
> Can prosecutors use a conviction for enhancement purposes more than one time? Check the Penal Code.
>
> When can punishment be enhanced for crimes committed because of bias or prejudice?
>
> What happens when a corporation or association is convicted of a crime? How is a business entity punished under the Texas Penal Code?

FINAL COMMENTS ON THE NATURE, ORIGINS, AND PURPOSES OF CRIMINAL LAW

The criminal law is society's last resort for exercising social control. It offers the most extreme and powerful set of sanctions. It is important to think about that power as you study the elements of various offenses and the grounds for various defenses. The State can exercise enormous influence over its citizens. Criminal defendants face the most serious of threats to their lives, liberties, and pocket books. The study of criminal law will not feel like a Perry Mason show. It will be exact and sometimes tedious. Details of offenses are important. Shades of meaning in interpreting the law are critical. It may seem as if courts are splitting hairs over the definitions of words and phrases. In the background, however, is the power of the State. When is the exercise of that power appropriate? Under what circumstances do we as a society want the State to take away an individual's freedom? What is the best punishment for a particular offense? Hard questions. No easy answers.

MULTIPLE CHOICE QUESTIONS

1. Serious bodily injury as defined in the Texas Penal Code would include:

    a. any injury that results in the victim's hospitalization.
    b. any and all harm to the victim's body.
    c. loss of limbs or permanent disfigurement.
    d. only injuries that are of a permanent nature.

2. Public servants as defined by the Penal Code do not include:

    a. jurors.
    b. persons performing governmental functions under a claim of right even though they are not legally qualified to do so.
    c. a college professor at a state university.
    d. employees of private companies that produce products for the U.S. military.

3. According to the Texas Penal Code, to possess something, a person:

    a. must actually have the object in his or her physical possession.
    b. can still possess an object even though it is not in his or her possession if they have a written agreement that states the object belongs to them.
    c. does not have to have actual physical possession of the object as long as they control how the object is used or what happens to it.
    d. can only possess an object if there is identifying marks or features on the object that allow it to be traced to that specific person.

4. Effective consent under the Penal Code would not include which of the following:

    a. a 12 year old child who allows his adult next door neighbor to take his family's car on a trip.
    b. a seriously mentally retarded woman who has a sexual relationship with a family friend.
    c. a man who agrees to commit a burglary with his friends because they have threatened to harm his sister if he fails to cooperate.
    d. all of the above.

5. Under the Texas Penal Code, assaulting a family member:

    a. is always punished the same way as assaulting a stranger.
    b. is punished less severely than assaulting a stranger because the offender is considered less of a risk to society at large.
    c. can be punished more severely than assaulting a stranger if the offender has a prior record of
    d. assaulting family members.
    e. is not considered a crime unless there is severe bodily injury to the family member.

6. Corporations in Texas:

    a. cannot be found guilty of criminal offenses.
    b. can be found guilty of offenses that provide for penalties consisting of only fines.
    c. can be found guilty of offenses that provide for imprisonment.
    d. can be found guilty of no greater than a third degree felony.

7. Aiding suicide in Texas:

    a. is not a crime.
    b. is a crime only if the person aided actually commits suicide.
    c. is no more than a Class C misdemeanor.
    d. can be a state jail felony if the aid causes suicide that results in serious bodily injury.

8. An offender can admit at the time of sentencing that he is guilty of another unadjudicated offense and request the court consider that offense in determining the sentence for the offense for which he has been adjudged guilty. If the court takes the unadjudicated offense into consideration:

    a. prosecution of the unadjudicated offense is prohibited.
    b. prosecution of the unadjudicated offense is not prohibited.
    c. the unadjudicated offense is deemed adjudged because of the offender's admission.
    d. the unadjudicated offense can have no bearing on the Judge's sentencing decision.

9. Criminal solicitation of a capital murder:

    a. is not a crime.
    b. is a second-degree felony if the murder never occurred.
    c. is a first-degree felony only if the murder occurred.
    d. is a first-degree felony.

10. A person found guilty of threatening to commit an act of violence to a another person with the intent to interrupt the public transportation system is guilty of a:

    a. a Class B misdemeanor.
    b. a Class A misdemeanor.
    c. a first-degree felony.
    d. a third-degree felony.

11. Wayne Wierdo had sent a letter to the headquarters of Texas Pharmacy Drugstore Co. stating that he intended to break into one of the company's 100 chain stores operated in Texas and put poison in some of the aspirin bottles sold on over the counter. If Wayne was apprehended by authorities before he was able to carry out his threat, he could be charged with a crime under the Texas Penal Code. What is the appropriate crime and its classification level?

    a. tampering with a consumer product, third-degree felony
    b. terroristic threat, third-degree felony
    c. deadly conduct, Class A misdemeanor
    d. tampering with a consumer product, first-degree felony

12. Bad Boy Blue went on a rampage against his archenemy and destroyed his enemy's favorite hot rod, smashing it with a tire iron. The damage amounted to $8000.00. Blue is facing:

    a. third-degree felony
    b. first-degree felony
    c. state jail felony
    d. second-degree felony

13. Joe, the serial burglar, decided to make several hits in one night. First, he burglarized the neighborhood shoe warehouse. A few hours later, he burglarized the residence of a wealthy lawyer. Joe was apprehended by the police. He could be charged with:

    a. state jail felony and a second-degree felony
    b. two second-degree felonies
    c. two state jail felonies
    d. a first and a second-degree felony

14. Timothy Trespasser could not stay away from "visiting" the downtown homeless shelter without the permission of the shelter authorities. Timothy was not homeless and did not want to spend the night. He was nosey. Timothy is guilty of:

    a. a third-degree felony
    b. a Class A misdemeanor
    c. a Class B misdemeanor
    d. no crime because it is not illegal to trespass a homeless shelter

15. Timothy also liked to remove railroad rails and use them as support beams for his cabin in the woods. The railroad company estimated that a rail is worth $300.00 For each rail he stole, Timothy could be charged with:

    a. a Class C misdemeanor
    b. a Class B misdemeanor
    c. a Class A misdemeanor
    d. no crime since no one has been injured and the rails are out in the public

CHAPTER TWO

CONSTITUTIONAL LIMITS ON CRIMINAL LAW

INTRODUCTION

Most constitutional challenges are based on the U.S. Constitution. State courts, however, can interpret state constitutions as giving citizens of that state more rights than are provided under the federal constitution. More and more frequently, appellants are arguing that their rights under a state constitution have been violated. Often, an appellant's argument is based on both the federal and state constitutions.

This chapter discusses some of the more common constitutional challenges to criminal statutes and examines pertinent sections of the Texas Constitution that impact on the constitutionality of criminal statutes. It relates sections of the state constitution to parallel clauses in the U.S. Constitution. For each section of the state constitution, the discussion also looks at recent cases decided by Texas courts, and a few from the U.S. Supreme Court, that have interpreted that section. The constitutional provisions discussed include:

(1) the ex post facto clause
(2) the equal protection clause
(3) void-for-vagueness and freedom of speech
(4) void-for-vagueness and due process

THE EX POST FACTO CLAUSE

Article I, section 16 of the Texas State Constitution states: "No bill of attainder, ex post facto law, retroactive law, or any law impairing the obligation of contracts, shall be made."

Section 16 parallels Article I, section 9 of the U.S. Constitution, which forbids the enactment of bills of attainder and ex post facto laws. A bill of attainder is a legislative act that inflicts punishment without a judicial determination. In a bill of attainder, the legislature decides an individual is guilty without any of the protective safeguards extended in a trial, such as representation by an attorney and rules of evidence. The framers of the Constitution were especially sensitive to bills of attainder because the British used them extensively before and during the American Revolution. The British Parliament would charge an individual with treason, pronounce his penalty, and confiscate his estate.

An ex post facto law makes an action that was innocent and performed before the passage of the law subject to criminal sanctions. The ex post facto clause also prohibits laws that aggravate a crime or make it greater than it was when it was committed; that change the punishment and inflict a greater punishment than what was provided at the time the crime was committed; and which change the rules of evidence than the law required at the time of the commission of the offense, making it easier to convict the offender.

Cases Interpreting the Ex Post Facto Clause

The reason for prohibiting ex post facto laws is imbedded in our history, however, the clause is far from being only of historic interest. It is alive and spawning new and creative grounds for appeals in criminal cases. Appellants who challenge their convictions under the ex post facto clause generally bring the challenge under both federal and state constitutions because, for the most part, both constitutions provide the same type and level of protection.

U.S. Supreme Court Cases

In 1997, the U.S. Supreme Court decided two important cases involving the ex post facto clause. In the first case, *Lynce v. Mathis*, 519 U.S. 443, 117 S.Ct. 891 (1997), the issue involved Florida statutes that authorized the award of early release "provisional" credits to prison inmates when the state prison population exceeded predetermined levels. In 1992, the Florida legislature canceled such credits for certain classes of inmates, including those convicted of murder or attempted murder. Kenneth Lynce was convicted of attempted murder in 1986 and received a 22 year prison sentence. He was released in 1992 after accumulating early release credits; including credits awarded as a result of prison overcrowding. Shortly after his release, the state attorney general issued an opinion interpreting the 1992 statute as having retroactively canceled all provisional credits awarded to inmates convicted of murder and attempted murder. Lynce was rearrested and returned to prison. He argued that the 1992 statute violated the ex post facto clause of the U.S. Constitution.

The Supreme Court held in Lynce's favor. It held that the 1992 state statute was clearly retrospective and disadvantaged Lynce by increasing his punishment even though the credits had been issued as a way to alleviate prison overcrowding. The motivation behind the award of credits was irrelevant. The Court relied heavily on a prior case it had decided concerning good time credits. In *Weaver v. Graham*, 450 U.S. 24 (1981), the Court ruled that a Florida law violated the ex post facto clause because it retroactively decreased the amount of good time available to an inmate who had been receiving a more generous amount of good time under the law in effect at the time of his conviction. By curtailing the availability of future credits, applying the new good time laws to the inmate postponed his eligibility for parole. It made the punishment for crimes committed before its enactment more onerous.

The second case decided by the Supreme Court in 1997 involving the ex post facto clause was *Kansas v. Hendricks*, 521 U.S. 346, 117 S.Ct. 2072 (1997), which concerned an offender convicted of child molestation with a long history of violent sex offenses. Right before he was to be released from prison, Kansas enacted the Sexually Violent Predator Act that provided for involuntary civil commitment of persons who due to a mental abnormality or personality disorder are likely to engage in predatory acts of sexual violence. Kansas filed a petition to civilly commit Hendricks under the new law after he was released from prison. He argued that the application of the law was in violation of the ex post facto clause because it resulted in the extension of his confinement and was punitive in nature. The U. S. Supreme disagreed and ruled against

Hendricks. The Court found that the state statute did not establish criminal proceedings and was not intended to punish. Since it was a civil proceeding that had no punitive purpose or result, the ex post facto clause was not implicated.

The United States Supreme Court recently examined Washington State's Community Protection Act, which similar to Kansas law, authorizes civilly committing violent sexual predators if their mental abnormality or personality disorder makes them likely to engage in sexual violence. Young challenged his commitment on the grounds that the state statute was punitive *as it was applied to him* because the conditions under which he was confined were punitive in effect. Because he was being subjected to punishment, not treatment, he asserted that the law violated the ex post facto clause. In the case *Seling v. Young,* ---- U.S. ---- (2001), the Court rejected Young's claim and decided that a civil statute cannot be considered punitive as applied to a single individual so as to violate the ex post facto clause. If individuals committed under the law want to challenge the conditions under which they are held, the Court stated they should pursue a lawsuit to improve their confinement conditions.

Another recent case decided by the U.S. Supreme Court involved a Texas man who was convicted on 15 counts of committing sexual offenses against his stepdaughter from 1991 to 1995, when she was 12 to 16 years old. Before September 1, 1993, the Texas Code of Criminal Procedure, section 38.07, provided that a victim's testimony about a sexual offense could not support a conviction unless it was corroborated by other evidence or if the victim informed another person of the offense within six months of when it occurred. The law provided an exception to the rule if the victim was under 14 years of age at the time of the offense, in which case, the victim's testimony alone could support a conviction. In 1993, the state legislature amended section 38.07, to allow a victim's testimony alone to support a conviction if the victim was under age 18. Carmell challenged four of his convictions by arguing that they could not stand under the pre-1993 version of the law that was in effect at the time of his conduct. Those four convictions were based solely on the victim's testimony and she was not under 14 at the time of the offense. In *Carmell v. Texas,* --- U.S. ---- (2001), the Supreme Court overruled the Texas courts and held that the four convictions could not stand under the ex post facto clause of the U.S. Constitution. In 1993, the state altered the rules of evidence for sexual assault convictions involving minors. Without the new rules, the state could not have convicted Carmell of those four counts. The Court held that the rules should not be applied to him because they were not the law when Carmell engaged in the behavior that was the basis for those particular counts.

Texas Court Cases

In *French v. State*, 830 S.W. 2d 607 (Tex.Crim.App. 1992), the Texas Court of Criminal Appeals considered instructions that were given to a jury that had convicted Mr. French of attempted murder and was to decide his sentence. Pursuant to a Texas law that went into effect after French committed his crime, the jury was advised that good time credit and parole do exist, but during their deliberations, they were not permitted to consider the manner in which the parole law might be applied to the defendant. French argued that the new law violated the ex post facto clause because it tainted the jury during their sentencing deliberations against his interests. The Texas Criminal Appeals Court did not agree and ruled against French.

The Texas Court of Appeals did not agree with Vernon Cooper in *Cooper v. State*, 2 S.W.3d 500 (Tex. App. – Texarkana 2000). Mr. Cooper was convicted of indecency with a child and placed on community supervision on deferred adjudication without having to plead guilty. When he failed to live up to several requirements of the sex offender registration act, his sentence was revoked, he was deemed guilty by the court and placed on regular community supervision. He argued that the sex offender registration requirements were not in effect when he committed his crime. The appeals court ruled that the requirements were not punishment and, therefore, there were no problems with the ex post facto clause.

Exercise:

Rogelio Cannady was convicted of two murders in 1991 and assessed two life sentences. While incarcerated for those murders, he killed a fellow inmate in October 1993. The State charged him with capital murder under a newly amended statute that aggravated his prison murder to a capital crime, Texas Penal Code, section 19.03 (a)(6):

(a) A person commits an offense if he commits murder as defined under Section 19.02(a)(1) of this code and:
(6) the person, while serving a sentence of life imprisonment or a term of 99 years for the commission of any offense listed in Section 3g(a)(1), Article 42.12, Code of Criminal Procedure, murders another.

Cannady argued that although the amendment that enhanced his prison homicide to a capital crime was effective September 1, 1993, the legislature provided that for the purposes of the law, an offense is committed before the effective date of the act if <u>any</u> element of the offense occurred before the effective date. Since he was incarcerated for two murders committed in 1991, they occurred prior to the effective date of the amended law. His conviction for capital murder should be barred. How do you think the Texas Court of Appeals in Corpus Christi ruled? See *State v. Cannady*, 913 S.W.2d 741 (Tex. App. - Corpus Christi 1996).

THE EQUAL PROTECTION CLAUSE

Article 1, section 3a of the Texas Constitution states: "Equality under the law shall not be denied or abridged because of sex, color, creed, or national origin. "

Article 1, section 3a parallels the equal protection clause found in the Fourteenth Amendment of the U.S. Constitution. Section 3a was added to the Texas Constitution in 1972. When a challenge is made to a criminal statute based on the equal protection clause, the Texas courts begin with the presumption that the purpose of the statute is constitutional. If the statute does not impinge on fundamental rights or does not involve a suspect classification, the burden of proof is on the party challenging the statute to show that the classification created by the law is not rationally related to a legitimate state interest. This is a heavy burden, and the courts are careful to examine what interest a statute is designed to serve and whether it actually serves that purpose.

Cases Interpreting the Equal Protection Clause

Smith v. State, 898 S.W.2d 838 (Tex. Crim. App. 1995), is an interesting and important case in the equal protection area. Defendant Smith was convicted of capital murder and sentenced to death. At the time of his conviction, under Texas law, parole was not a matter for jury consideration in a capital murder trial. When the jury assessed punishment, they were not informed that a defendant convicted of capital murder and given a life sentence was not eligible for parole and must serve a 40-year sentence. Smith contended that Texas law violated both the equal protection clauses of the U.S. and Texas Constitutions because juries trying non-capital cases are given information about the possibility of parole. He alleged that Texas law created a separate classification for capital murder offenders that did not serve a legitimate state interest. He argued that Texas jurors are asked during punishment deliberations whether the defendant represents a continuing threat to society. Without knowing that a life sentence means no eligibility for parole for at least 40 years, the jury must answer that question without knowing all the legal consequences of a capital murder life sentence.

The Texas Court of Criminal Appeals rejected Smith's contention because they determined that a classification is not illegitimate if it does not discriminate against similarly situated individuals. In Smith's case, he was treated differently than offenders who are convicted of non-capital crimes, but they are not similarly situated individuals. He was treated exactly the same as every other defendant convicted of capital murder. During the sentencing phase, none of those defendants were able to introduce evidence concerning the lack of parole eligibility for capital murderers.

Soon after the *Smith* decision, the Texas legislature responded to mounting pressure to change what many saw as a fundamentally unfair law. Effective for homicides committed after September 1, 1999, the amended Texas statute requires the judge to inform the jury during the punishment phase of a capital murder trial that if the defendant is sentenced to imprisonment instead of death, he or she will not be eligible for parole until they have served 40 years without any good time credit.

Finley was convicted of attempted rape and made the argument in *Finley v. State*, 527 S.W.2d 553 (Tex. Crim. App. 1975), that the rape laws in effect at the time were unconstitutional under the state constitution's equal protection clause. He argued that section 3a prohibited a statute that constrains men but not women. The rape laws were written in such a way that only a man could be found guilty of perpetrating the crime. The Texas court admitted that the laws set up a classification on the basis of sex. The judges decided that the rape laws served a legitimate state interest. They reasoned that men perpetrate most sexual assaults against women; the state has an interest in preventing unwanted pregnancies; and there are other provisions of the Penal Code to protect men from sexual assaults by women. Finley's argument was ahead of its time. Several years after his case was decided, the state legislature created sexual assault statutes that are gender neutral.

Exercise:
Vernon Ellis was convicted of aggravated assault. He argued that the Texas Government Code section 62.106 and 62.108 violated the section 3a of the Texas Constitution because they allow individuals over 65 to be exempted from jury service. According to Ellis, the exemption deprived him of a jury panel that was representative of a fair cross-section of his community. How did the Texas Court of Appeals in Dallas analyze the legislative classification concerning jury service based on age? See *Weaver v. State*, 823 S.W.2d 371 (Tex. App. - Dallas 1992).

VOID-FOR-VAGUENESS AND FREEDOM OF SPEECH

Article 1, section 8 of the Texas Constitution states: "Every person shall be at liberty to speak, write or publish his opinions on any subject, being responsible for the abuse of that privilege; and no law shall ever be passed curtailing the liberty of speech or of the press. In prosecutions for the publications of papers, investigating the conduct of officers, or men in public capacity, or when the matter published is proper for public information, the truth thereof may be given in evidence. And in all indictments for libels, the jury shall have the right to determine the law and the facts, under the direction of the court, as in other cases."

Article 8 parallels the part of the First Amendment of the U.S. Constitution that addresses freedom of speech. Texas has explicitly guaranteed the freedom of Texans to write, publish and speak ever since the Constitution of the Republic of Texas, dating back to 1836.

Criminal laws must be sufficiently clear to give a person of ordinary intelligence a reasonable opportunity to know what is prohibited and to establish guidelines for law enforcement. When issues of freedom of speech are involved, criminal laws must also be sufficiently definite to avoid chilling protected expression. In fact, when a criminal statute is capable of affecting freedom of speech and expression, the courts examine extra carefully the degree of specificity found in the statute. The U.S. Supreme Court held in *Gooding v. Wilson*, 405 U.S. 518, 92 S.Ct. 1103 (1972) that when a void-for-vagueness challenge involves First Amendment considerations, a criminal law may be held invalid even though it may <u>not</u> be unconstitutional as applied to the defendant's particular conduct

Cases Interpreting Freedom of Speech and Vagueness

In *Long v. State*, 931 S.W.2d 285 (Tex. Crim. App. 1996), the Texas Court of Criminal Appeals reviewed the stalking provisions of the 1993 Texas harassment statute, Texas Penal Code, section 42.07 (a)(7), for possible void-for-vagueness problems. The stalking portion of the law provided:

> (a) A person commits an offense if, with intent to harass, annoy, alarm, abuse, torment, or embarrass another, he:
> (7)(A) on more than one occasion engages in conduct directed specifically toward the other person, including following that person, that is reasonably likely to harass, annoy, alarm, abuse, torment, or embarrass that person;
> (B) on at least one of those occasions by acts or words threatens to inflict bodily injury on that person or to commit an offense against that person, a member of that person's family, or that person's property; and
> (C) on at least one of those occasions engages in conduct after the person toward whom the conduct is specifically directed has reported to a law enforcement agency the conduct described by this subdivision.

(e) It is an affirmative defense to prosecution under Subsection (a)(7) of this section that the actor was engaged in conduct that consisted of activity in support of constitutionally or statutorily protected rights.

Long contended that section (a)(7)(A) was vague and rendered the entire statute unconstitutional. The Texas court agreed. The court was concerned that words like "harass," "annoy" and "alarm" are susceptible to uncertainties of meaning. Requiring the conduct to be "specifically directed" toward a particular person failed to limit the expansive coverage of the conduct. Requiring the conduct to be "reasonably likely to harass …" also failed to limit the expansive reach of the law. The reporting requirement in (a)(7)(C) and the threat requirement in (a)(7)(B) did not remove the First Amendment concerns. Interestingly, Texas' prior harassment statute was also held unconstitutional because of vagueness in the case *Kramer v. Price*, 712 F.2d 174 (5th Cir. 1983).

A Houston city ordinance was at issue in *Haddad v. State*, 9 S.W.3d 454 (Tex.App.-Houston [1st Dist.] 1999). The ordinance made it unlawful for any entertainer to touch a customer or the customer's clothing while entertaining or exposing any specified anatomical areas or engaging in specified sexual activities. The ordinance defined "specified anatomical areas" and "specified sexual activities." Haddad was a topless dancer who was charged with intentionally touching a customer while she was dancing. She alleged that the ordinance was void-for-vagueness. The court disagreed. Neither did the court agree that the ordinance reached into constitutionally protected conduct. Topless dancing is protected by freedom of speech under the Texas constitution, however, the state is free to place time, place, and manner restrictions that help protect the welfare of customers and dancers.

Exercise:
Defendant Brian Jacobs told Police Officer Edwards "when I get out I'm coming to your house to kill you and your family." Jacobs plead guilty to attempted retaliation, a Class A misdemeanor. On appeal, he complained that his conviction violated his right to free speech under the U.S. and Texas Constitutions. Read the retaliation statute in the Texas Penal Code. Do you think it abridges constitutionally protected speech? To see what the court decided, find the case *Jacobs v. State*, 903 S.W.2d 848 (Tex. App. – Texarkana 1995).

VOID-FOR-VAGUENESS AND DUE PROCESS

Article 1, section 19 of the Texas Constitution states: "No citizen of this State shall be deprived of life, liberty, property, privileges, or immunities or in any manner disenfranchised, except by the due course of the law of the land."

Article 19 parallels the due process clause of the Fourteenth Amendment of the U.S. Constitution. In addition to providing procedural due process, Article 19 also requires substantive due process, laws and their enforcement may not be arbitrary, unreasonable, or unrelated to a legitimate concern of the state.

Defendants who challenge a criminal statute as vague under the due process clause of either the Texas or U.S. Constitutions must show that the operation of the statute is unconstitutional <u>to him or her in their situation</u>. Unlike challenges of vagueness under the First

Amendment and Article 1, section 8 of the Texas Constitution, the fact that the statute may be unconstitutional as applied to other persons is not sufficient. A criminal statute is vague when persons of common intelligence must guess at its meaning and differ about how it should be applied. The language of a statute is not unconstitutionally vague if it conveys a sufficient warning about the proscribed conduct, as measured by common understanding and practices. Words in a statute are to be read in context and construed according to the rules of grammar and common usage. The word or terms in a statute do not have to be specifically defined.

Much like the freedom of speech and vagueness inquiry, under the due process clause the first issue is whether an ordinary, law-abiding person is put sufficiently on notice by a criminal statute that his or her conduct violated the law. The second issue is whether the statute gave sufficient notice to law enforcement authorities to prevent arbitrary or discriminating enforcement.

Cases Interpreting Vagueness and Due Process

Denise McCarty argued in her case *McCarty v. State*, 616 S.W.2d 194 (Tex. Crim. App. 1981), that the Texas statute prohibiting prostitution was unconstitutional because it was so vaguely worded. Section 43.02(a)(1) of the Texas Penal Code stated:

(a) A person commits an offense if he knowingly:
(1) offers to engage, agrees to engage, or engages in sexual conduct for a fee

McCarty alleged that the word "offer" was so vague it did not give fair warning of what is illegal conduct, violating the due process clause.

The Texas Court of Criminal Appeals noted that the prohibition against excessive vagueness does not invalidate every statute a court believes could have been drafted more precisely. Due process requires only that a law give sufficient warning to allow people to conduct themselves so as to avoid unlawful behavior, and that a law not lull people into a false sense of security. The court concluded that the Texas law gave people sufficient warning of what is prohibited, and the word "offer" is not so vague as to raise speculation about its meaning.

J.D. Parr made a similar argument against the involuntary manslaughter statute, section 19.05(a)(2) of the Texas Penal Code. In *Parr v. State*, 575 S.W.2d 522 (Tex. Crim. App. 1979), Parr argued that his conviction for involuntary manslaughter should be reversed because the statute as then written failed to define intoxication sufficiently to avoid vagueness problems. Parr struck and killed a child while driving his car while intoxicated. A blood sample revealed that his blood contained .23 percent alcohol.

Parr challenged the definition of intoxication on the grounds that the wording of the law condemned the voluntary introduction of *any* substance into the body and failed to give notice as to which substances are prohibited. He contended the statute might prohibit the driving of an automobile while a person is voluntarily taking prescription medicine. The statute stated that:

For purposes of this section, 'intoxication' means that the actor does not have the normal use of his mental or physical faculties by reason of the voluntary introduction of any substance into his body.

The court ruled that the statute was not unconstitutional. Its focus was not on the type of substances a person ingests. It condemned voluntarily introducing any substance, even legal ones, that caused a person to loose the normal use of mental or physical faculties while operating a motor vehicle and which then resulted in the death of another person.

> **Exercise:**
> Raul Naranjo was convicted of possessing an inhalant. He challenged the constitutionality of Chapters 484 and 485 of the Texas Health and Safety Code on the grounds that they are vague. Section 484.003 provides a criminal penalty for possessing and using certain volatile chemicals. Section 485.031 provides a criminal penalty for possessing and using abusable glues and aerosol paints. Naranjo claimed that the sections violated the Constitution because a defendant charged under them is unable to determine which statute is more applicable. Read Chapters 484 and 485 of the Health and Safety Code. How did the Texas Court of Appeals rule? See *Naranjo v. State*, 890 S.W.2d 467 (Tex. App. - Corpus Christi 1994).
>
> Notice that not all criminal statutes are found in the Penal Code!

FINAL COMMENTS ON THE CONSTITUTIONAL LIMITS ON THE CRIMINAL LAW

Constitutional issues are important issues in many criminal cases; however, they are not present in the majority of cases. Nonetheless, it is essential you understand the constitutional provisions, state and federal, which impact the drafting and interpretation of criminal law. The failure of a law to past constitutional muster often results in very serious consequences for the State. Courts obligated to uphold the constitution can strike down well-intentioned legislation. Legislatures must be aware of the constitutional ramifications of the laws they adopt. By understanding the state and federal constitutional provisions, you can better appreciate the decisions courts are sometimes forced to make.

MULTIPLE CHOICE QUESTIONS

1. The Texas Constitution, as interpreted by the Texas courts, cannot give the citizens of Texas greater protections than those afforded by the U.S. Constitution.

    a. True
    b. False

2. The Texas Constitution, as interpreted by the Texas courts, can reduce the rights afforded to citizens in Texas from those afforded by similar provisions of the U.S. Constitution.

    a. True
    b. False

3. The equal protection clause requires that:

   a. all persons in the state be treated exactly the same under all circumstances.
   b. Texans must be treated the same, but citizens from other states can be treated differently.
   c. persons in similarly situated circumstances must be treated similarly.
   d. every citizen is protected equally from arbitrary criminal prosecution.

4. The Constitution prevented the state of Florida from taking away Lynce's good time credits awarded because of prison overcrowding because:

   a. Florida was violating the equal protection clause by treating its prisoners differently than other states.
   b. the state statute was so vague as to makes its provisions debatable.
   c. due process required that taking away credits be done after a hearing.
   d. the retraction of his credits violated the ex post facto clause.

5. The Constitution did not require that Kansas strike down its Sexually Violent Predator Act even though it resulted in the further confinement of certain predatory violent sex offenders because:

   a. the law did not violate the ex post facto clause because the confinement was civil not criminal in nature.
   b. the law did not violate the ex post facto clause because it did not apply to persons incarcerated before it went into effect.
   c. it did not violate the equal protection clause because all violent, predatory sex offenders are treated alike.
   d. it did not violate the equal protection clause because it creates a special class of sex offenders, which is reasonably related to a legitimate government purpose.

6. When courts examine laws that are allegedly void-for-vagueness and violate due process, they:

   a. strike down all laws that do not carefully define every word.
   b. assume that the laws are vague and put the burden on the government to prove they are not vague.
   c. assume that all laws are clear and easy to understand if only the citizens would read them more carefully.
   d. examine the law to see if it provides sufficient warning of the prohibited conduct, based on a common understanding.

7. When a void-for-vagueness challenge is made that a statute violates constitutionally protected freedom of speech, the courts:

    a. generally rule against the law.
    b. are willing to strike it down even if it is not unconstitutional as applied to the appellant in the particular case before the court.
    c. are unwilling to strike it down unless it is unconstitutional as applied to the particular appellant before the court.
    d. are mostly concerned with whether the law provides sufficient definitions of all the important terms.

8. The Texas and U.S. Constitutions have very different equal protection provisions.

    a. True
    b. False

9. The Texas courts are called upon and do interpret the constitutionality of Texas criminal laws under both the Texas and U.S. Constitutions.

    a. True
    b. False

10. As it currently stands, the Texas statute that prohibits capital juries from hearing about the parole laws applicable to convicted capital offenders is:

    a. unconstitutional because it violates the equal protection clause.
    b. unconstitutional because it violates the due process clause.
    c. constitutional because it does not violate the equal protection clause.
    d. constitutional because it applies only to offenders convicted of capital murder.

CHAPTER THREE

THE GENERAL PRINCIPLES OF CRIMINAL LIABILITY: THE REQUIREMENT OF ACTION

INTRODUCTION

This chapter looks at cases decided by Texas courts that have interpreted section 6.01 of the Texas Penal Code dealing with the voluntary act requirement. It might seem easy to prove that a criminal act was voluntary. Except for those few, unusual cases involving defendants who claim they acted while sleepwalking or were possessed by demons, what is there to voluntariness? Surprisingly, the issue can arise in cases that involve fairly direct and typical fact situations.

Section 6.01(a) of the Code provides that to be convicted of a crime, a person must have voluntarily engaged in the act, omission, or possession that constitutes the offense. The Code does not define "voluntary." Courts and juries have to struggle with deciding what is a voluntary act based on actual fact situations.

The voluntariness issue is often raised on appeal when the appellant contends that the trial judge failed to give instructions to the jury about voluntariness. The Texas Code of Criminal Procedure requires a judge to deliver a set of written instructions to the jury that outline the law applicable to the case they are deciding, without expressing an opinion about the weight of the evidence. Before these instructions or jury charge is read to the jury, defendant's counsel and the prosecution have the opportunity to review it and present objections. The objections can include protests about what is and what is not in the charge.

Without instructions specifically addressing voluntariness, jurors are required by law to assume the defendant's actions were voluntary. If the defendant is convicted, on appeal the voluntariness issue often gets tangled up with other issues involving the appellant's culpability - was the act performed intentionally, knowingly, recklessly, or negligently. In examining the facts for purposes of determining voluntariness, appellate courts frequently address the whole issue of blameworthiness. Whenever courts and judges delve into the human psyche, it is an imperfect, sometimes frustrating exercise. Remember that reasonable minds may differ.

I Didn't Mean to Do It!

Read the account of what happened in *George v. State*, 681 S.W.2d 43, 44 (Tex. Crim. App. 1984) in which appellant Bobby George was convicted of aggravated assault:

> On the late afternoon of a March day, thirteen-year-old Leonard Martin was visiting younger brothers of appellant in the home of appellant and other members of his family. Appellant was then seventeen. All present were friends. Standing in front of a seated Martin, appellant demanded a dollar from him; when the latter verbally refused to produce it appellant drew a .22 caliber revolver from a pocket, thumbed its hammer partially back and, pointing it at Martin's face, told Martin to "give me the dollar," the gun discharged, its bullet striking Martin in the left maxilla of his face ...... Appellant threw the gun aside, striking a brother in the chest; he went with Martin to the home of a neighbor to seek aid, but they were denied. At another house, however, an ambulance was summoned.
>
> In his confession and testimony at trial appellant described in greater detail that after he asked Martin a second time for a dollar he cocked the hammer back short of its locked position; that he "struck [the gun] up in [Martin's] face;" that Martin "turned his face away," that the "the hammer slipped off my thumb" and the gun "went off." Appellant further told the jury that he did not know the gun would nor did he mean for it to go off "when he cocked the hammer back;" he denied ever pulling the trigger and stated that he did not intend to shoot Martin or harm him in any way - it was an accident.

Bobby George wanted the trial judge to issue an instruction to the jury about the voluntariness requirement under section 6.01(a). The judge had only instructed the jury about intentionally, knowingly, or recklessly causing bodily injury to the victim under the aggravated assault statute. The Texas Court of Criminal Appeals held that if there is evidence that an act was performed accidentally, the jury should be instructed to consider whether the act was voluntary. Without saying so specifically, the court concluded that the defense of accident is found in section 6.01(a). The court went on to construe section 6.01(a) to mean that a person voluntarily engages in conduct when the conduct includes a voluntary act and its accompanying mental state. But here is where the court's holding gets tricky. Just because a person's conduct also includes an involuntary act does not necessarily mean that the person engaged in that conduct involuntarily. Nor is conduct involuntary merely because a person does not intend the result of his conduct.

When the court applied its holding to George's case, it concluded that George acted voluntarily in handling the gun. He acted voluntarily up to the second when he claimed that the hammer slipped off his thumb and the gun discharged. The gun did not discharge by accident. If the hammer slipped off George's thumb, the thumb holding the hammer released just enough pressure for the hammer to slip forward.

Contrast the *George* case to *Garcia v. State*, 605 S.W.2d 565, 566 (Tex. Crim. App. 1980). In *Garcia*, the Court of Criminal Appeals decided that the jury should have been instructed about the voluntariness of the appellant's conduct because there was evidence of an accident. The case reads:

Testifying in his own behalf, appellant related that the deceased gave him the gun as they were walking on the sidewalk and that the hammer was already pulled. When appellant told the deceased that he was going to throw the gun into the canal, the deceased suddenly grabbed appellant's right elbow with one hand and the gun with his other hand in an attempt to take the gun away from appellant. Appellant testified:

"Q. Okay. Now, at what point did the gun go off?
"A. When he pulled on the gun, tried to get it out of my hand.

* * * * * *

"Q. Okay. Did you have any intention or knowledge or any state of mind at all of the sort that would make you desire to harm Hector Jaimes (the deceased) in any way?

"A. No, sir."

Exercise:
Compare the alleged accident that occurred in the *George* case and the alleged accident that occurred in the *Garcia* case. What are the differences between the circumstances surrounding both shootings? If you believe the appellant's version of the facts in *George*, that he did not intend to harm Martin, why did the court conclude there was no evidence that his act was involuntary? What about the court's decision in *Garcia* is instructive with respect to the decision in *George*?

Voluntariness was also the issue in *Shugart v. State*, 796 S.W.2d 288 (Tex. App. - Beaumont 1990). Shugart was convicted of a misdemeanor assault after hitting the victim with his car, knocking her onto the hood. She slid off the hood and sustained back injuries. He failed to render assistance and drove away from the scene. Shugart is paralyzed from the chest down with no feeling in his legs. He argued that he had accidentally hit the victim when he inadvertently shifted the car into drive. The Court of Appeals refused to disturb the jury's verdict of guilt because there was ample evidence that the appellant had been hassling the victim prior to striking her with his automobile. There was also ample evidence that despite his paralysis he was a very skilled driver.

Exercise:
If the court had concluded in the *Shugart* case that Shugart inadvertently shifted the car into drive, what legal conclusion do you think the court would have reached?

Robert Cruz argued that he was not guilty of aggravated assault of a correctional officer because his actions were not voluntary in *Cruz v. State*, 838 S.W.2d 682 (Tex. App. - Houston [14th Dist.] 1992). Cruz was convicted of assaulting a correctional officer while fighting with several officers. The facts showed that during the altercation Cruz fell on top of an officer thereby dislocating the officer's shoulder. He maintained that he did not intend to harm the officer. The appeals court did not agree that the jury should have been instructed on the issue of voluntariness. The appellant set off the chain of events that led to the officer's injuries. Cruz may not have intended to cause injuries, but he voluntarily engaged in behavior that led to harm.

> **Exercise:**
> How are the *Cruz* and *George* cases alike? How are they different? In both cases the appellate court decided there was no evidence that the acts were involuntary. What about the appellants' actions in both cases impacted the courts' conclusions?

Phillip Rhodes was convicted of criminally negligent homicide after he ran a red light at an intersection and collided broadside with another car. At his trial, Rhodes testified that he did not see the red light. On appeal he argued that the judge should have given the jury a voluntariness instruction because he did not voluntarily participate in running a red light. The jury should have been permitted to consider whether his actions met the requirements of section 6.01. If it should decide that his actions were not voluntary, he is not criminally responsible for the results. The Texas Court of Appeals denied Rhodes' request in *Rhodes v. State*, 997 S.W.2d 692 (Tex. App. - Texarkana). The court concluded that Rhodes voluntarily failed to keep a proper lookout, which resulted in his not seeing a red light. There was no evidence that Rhodes' failure was involuntary.

I Was Compelled to Act

In *Alford v. State*, 866 S.W.2d 619 (Tex. Crim. App. 1993), the appellant was convicted of aggravated robbery. He argued that he was acting under duress and participated in the crime under threats of serious bodily harm. Duress is an affirmative defense in section 8.05 of the T.P.C., but the appellant argued that an act performed under duress was also an involuntary act under section 6.01(a). After an extensive review of the Penal Code, the court decided that voluntariness refers only to a person's physical bodily movements. The appellant cannot claim that an act committed under duress is not voluntary.

Shelly Ardis was convicted of possession of cocaine. Police stopped Ardis at 3:00 a.m. for driving her car the wrong way down a one-way street. Ardis pulled her car into a parking lot before she was stopped. She was the only passenger in the car, and the officer suspected she was intoxicated. When the officer asked, she indicated she wanted to drive home. Ardis complied when the officer asked her to get out of the automobile. The officer concluded she was intoxicated to the degree she was a danger to herself and others. He arrested her for public intoxication, and, in a search incident to the arrest, he found cocaine on her person. Ardis argued in *Ardis v. State*, 2001 LEXIS 22 (Tex. App.- Dallas 2001), that she should not have been arrested for public intoxication because she did not voluntarily get out of her car, and until she got out of her car she was not in a public place. If the arrest was not legal, the search was not legal. The appeals court did not agree. It concluded that Ardis exited her car so that the officer could decide whether to it was safe to release the car to her, which is what she had requested. Her actions were voluntary.

Possession

The actus reus of possession is defined in two different Code statutes. The Code's definition is located in section 1.07(38): possession means actual care, custody, control, or management. Ownership is not required, nor is it required that the item actually be on your person, as long as you are exercising care, control, or management over it. In section 6.01(b), possession is further defined as voluntary if the possessor knowingly obtained or received the item or was aware that he controlled the item for a sufficient time to permit him to terminate his control.

Possession often becomes an issue in cases involving illegal possession of drugs or possession of drugs with intent to distribute. In *Linton v. State*, 15 S.W.3d 615 (Tex. App.-Houston [14th] 2000), two Houston police officers stopped Linton for failure to display an inspection sticker on his vehicle. The officers conducted a background check and discovered that he had outstanding city warrants. He was arrested and his vehicle towed. During an inventory search, officers found a small glass pipe with burn marks and a chalky, white film inside it. When asked, Linton admitted the pipe was his. On appeal, Linton argued that there was insufficient evidence that he possessed cocaine long enough to allow him to terminate control over it.

The appeals court ruled against Linton and reviewed the status of the law in Texas. It held that the State has to prove two things when it charges someone with unlawful possession. First, it must show that the defendant exercised actual care, custody, control, or management over the contraband. Secondly, the State must prove the defendant knew the object he possessed was contraband. Without an admission of guilt, the knowledge element of the crime can be inferred and possession can be proved by circumstantial evidence. When contraband is not found on the defendant's person, or it is not in his or her exclusive possession, additional facts must affirmatively link the defendant to it. Those links can include: 1) evidence about whether the contraband was in plain view; 2) whether it was in close proximity to the defendant; 3) whether the amount of the substance was large enough to indicate the defendant knew of its presence; 4) whether the defendant owned or was closely related to the owner of the vehicle or residence where the substance was found and; 5) whether the defendant made furtive gestures. All the facts do not necessarily need to point directly or indirectly to the defendant's guilt. The evidence is sufficient if the combined and cumulative effect of all the incriminating circumstances point to the defendant's guilt.

In Linton's case, the court concluded there were sufficient affirmative links between him and the cocaine to indicate that he had a long enough time to terminate his control over it. He was the sole occupant and driver of the car where it was found. It was located in the center console, in close proximity to him. The cocaine was in a glass pipe that was in plain view next to Linton's wallet in the console and could be observed from the passenger seat. Linton admitted that it was his pipe. There was evidence he controlled the pipe and knew of its presence.

The court reached a similar conclusion in *Luke v. State*, 2001 Tex. App. LEXIS 652 (Tex. App.- Houston [14th] 2001). In that case, Luke had been under surveillance by undercover narcotics officers who had information that he was selling cocaine. They followed him to a school where he picked up his girlfriend after work. He was driving his girlfriend's car. When she came out to meet him, he got out of the car from the driver's seat and moved to the passenger side. His girlfriend sat in the driver's seat and drove off. At that point, police pulled him over. As an officer approached the vehicle, he saw Luke look left and right and move something with his left hand. After the officer removed Luke from the car and handcuffed him, the officer found a baggy with rock cocaine where Luke's hand had been. Luke argued on appeal that there was insufficient evidence linking him to possession of cocaine. The court did not agree. Not only was he in close proximity to the cocaine, he exercised sole control over the automobile until just a few minutes before he was stopped, and he was closely related to the owner. Police observed him making furtive gestures as they approached him.

Omission

Section 6.01 provides that a person who omits to perform an act does not commit an offense unless there is a law that makes it a crime to omit to act or provides that a person has the duty to perform the act. "Omission" is defined by section 1.07 as the failure to act. There are very few laws that require a person to perform an act. Crimes of omission are not everyday offenses.

Section 22.04 makes it a crime to intentionally, knowingly, or recklessly by omission cause injury, mental deficiency or impairment to a child, elderly person, or a disabled person, if you had a legal duty to act or had assumed the care, custody, or control of that person. Section 22.041 makes it a crime to intentionally, knowingly, recklessly, or with criminal negligence by omission place a child younger than 15 in imminent danger of death, injury, or physical or mental impairment. Section 25.05 creates the crime of criminal nonsupport, which makes it a legal duty for a person to provide financial support for his or her child under age 18 or for a child who is the subject of a court order requiring support. A new statute, section 38.17, makes it a class A misdemeanor to fail to stop or to report aggravated sexual assault of a child even if the person did not assume care, custody, or control of the child as defined in section 22.04.

Laws that require certain acts be performed are not always located in the Penal Code. John Dennis Moore appealed from a jury conviction for failure to register as a sex offender under Chapter 62 of the Texas Code of Criminal Procedure. Moore had been convicted of Indecency With a Child in 1993 and was sentenced to prison. He was released on mandatory supervision in 1998. His parole officer advised him that he had a duty to register as a convicted sex offender under a law that went into effect September 1, 1997. Moore argued that he should not have to register because failure to register is a crime of omission under section 6.01 and requires a statutory duty to register as an element of the offense. Since he was convicted in 1993, his conviction is an element of the crime of failure to register as a sex offender that occurred prior to September 1, 1997. The court ruled that it was Moore's status as a convicted sex offender rather than his prior conviction that was an element of the offense of failure to register. The State's burden was to prove Moore's status as a person with a reportable conviction at the time he failed to register, not that the date he was convicted was later than September 1, 1997.

> **Exercises:**
> Read *Bidelspach v. State*, 840 S.W.2d 516 (Tex. App. - Dallas 1992) concerning a city ordinance that prohibits the transportation of liquid waste without a valid permit and an ordinance that requires anyone who transports liquid waste to complete a trip ticket for each location served. What does the case say about crimes of omission?
>
> Read *Hawkins v. State*, 891 S.W.2d 257 (Tex. Crim. App. 1994). Hawkins was convicted of injury to a child under the T.P.C. section 22.04. He was the live-in boyfriend of Theresa Hutchins, the infant victim's biological mother. The evidence showed that on four occasions, Hutchins beat her child in the presence of Hawkins. He did not try to prevent the attacks or seek to remove the child from the mother during the attacks. The State accused Hawkins of injury to the infant by alleging he had a legal duty to remove the child because he had assumed care, custody, and control of the child. The intermediate appellate court ruled that Hawkins did not have a legal duty to remove the child. How you think the Texas Court of Criminal Appeals ruled in this case?

FINAL COMMENTS ON THE ACTUS REUS REQUIREMENT

The actus reus of a crime must be proved beyond a reasonable doubt. In cases where voluntariness, possession, or omission is the issue, the State's burden can be difficult. The law allows the jury to make reasonable inferences based on circumstantial evidence in those instances where direct evidence is missing or in dispute. Without the ability to reach reasonable conclusions using circumstantial evidence many cases would never go to trial and many offenders would never be punished. On the other hand, the reasonable doubt standard protects the individual from overreaching or unreasonable inferences based on evidence that is too speculative or tangential. It is a delicate balance sometimes that requires sound judgment and a genuine concern that justice be done.

MULTIPLE CHOICE QUESTIONS

1. Possession can be an act under the Penal Code:

    a. even if the possessor is not aware of what he or she possesses.
    b. only if the possessor knowingly receives the thing possessed.
    c. only if the possessor refuses to rid himself or herself of the item.
    d. if the possessor actually has the contraband item on his person or among his possessions.

2. Jerry kept his stash of marijuana in his briefcase. When the police entered the apartment he shared with a friend (located in Waco, Texas) with a search warrant to look for illegal drugs, his briefcase was in the living room. They asked if they could open it up and Jerry consented to the search. Of course, the police discovered the marijuana and arrested Jerry who acknowledged that the pot was his. Jerry alleged that even though he admitted to owning the marijuana he did not possess it and, therefore, was not guilty.

a. Jerry is correct. He is not guilty because the pot was not on his person.
   b. Jerry would have been ok if he just hadn't admitted that the pot belonged to him.
   c. Jerry has an uphill battle because the pot was found in his briefcase in his apartment.
   d. Jerry isn't guilty because the pot was for his personal use.

3. Smithie was an insulin-dependent diabetic who was supposed to take 3 shots of insulin a day. Smithie was careless about taking her medication and would often forget it. Other times she would decide she didn't want to take a shot – no matter how important it was. Last week, Smithie decided to ignore her insulin and went without it for a couple of days. She was driving an automobile when she hit and killed a pedestrian who was walking across the street in a crosswalk zone. She argued that she was not guilty because her vision was very blurry and she didn't even see the pedestrian. Doctors testified that her blurry vision was a result of not taking insulin.

   a. Smithie's right – her poor vision resulted from a medical condition.
   b. Smithie's crazy – this is a strict liability offense.
   c. Smithie voluntarily chose not to take her insulin and is responsible for what resulted from that decision.
   d. Smithie did not want to harm anyone and is not guilty.

4. Doris hated her sister Karen for stealing her husband. It didn't help that Karen was also a successful ballerina with a major ballet company and Doris had two left feet. Doris hoped that someday something terrible would happen to Karen as pay back. During a family reunion, Karen and Doris found themselves alone together on the family boat in the middle of a large lake. They started to argue. Karen got so upset that she stood up in the boat and threw her arms around in a crazy motion. Suddenly, she slipped and fell into the water. Doris, an accomplished swimmer, watched her drown, smiling as Karen's body went down for the last time.

   a. Doris was obligated to try to save a family member and is guilty of a criminal act of omission.
   b. Doris was obligated to try to save anyone who she voluntarily chose to be in a boat with because she had assumed that person's care.
   c. Doris was within her legal right not to assist her sister.
   d. Doris may or may not be guilty depending on whether she realized how serious Karen's situation was.

5. Sally and her husband decided to take an elderly man into their home because he was unable to care for himself. He wasn't seriously ill, but he was unable to prepare meals for himself and clean his clothes regularly. Sally and her husband agreed to provide him a bedroom, meals, and clean his clothes in exchange for a portion of his Social Security check. What the elderly man didn't realize was that Sally and her husband were only interested in his money, not in his care. They often failed to feed him, and he never received a good meal when they did prepare food. His health deteriorated significantly, to the point that neighbors called the police.

a. Sally and her husband may be guilty under section 22.04 of the T.P.C. as long as their elderly tenant was over 65.
   b. Sally and her husband may be guilty under 22.04 no matter how old their tenant is because they assumed his care.
   c. Sally and her husband breached a contract, no more than that.
   d. Sally and her husband are not guilty because the elderly man was not seriously ill and had the ability to move out if things were that bad.

6. Kenneth was an experienced drug dealer. He decided that instead of transporting drugs on his person or in containers that he would carry, it was safer to have someone carry the drugs for him. That way, if the police busted the other person, he could keep a distance. Kenneth had ways to terrify the person into not snitching on him in the event they were arrested. One day, Kenneth arranged for Stevie to carry a stash of cocaine across town to a purchaser. Kenneth shadowed Stevie along the way to make certain that the delivery was made as planned. The police stopped Stevie who was acting nervous and confused. During a legal stop, they asked a few questions that raised their suspicions even more. They asked Stevie for permission to search him, and he agreed. They found the cocaine and arrested him. As he was being arrested, Stevie pointed to Kenneth who was lurking in the bushes nearby.

   a. Kenneth did not have possession of illegal drugs and the State has no case.
   b. Kenneth could argue that even if he owned the cocaine, he didn't possess it at the time Stevie was searched.
   c. If the State can gather enough evidence to show the connection between Kenneth and Stevie, Kenneth may have serious legal problems because Kenneth had control of the cocaine even while it was in Stevie's possession.
   d. Kenneth can easily argue successfully that once he gave the coke to Stevie to transport, he lost control over it because Stevie could have dashed into a waiting car or taxi and fled with the drugs if he had chosen to.

7. Terry refused to cut his grass and his yard was in shambles. This angered the neighbors who all had lovely yards and gardens. They called the police, alleging that Terry was failing to abide by the terms of a homeowners' agreement. Every homeowner signed the agreement in the neighborhood, including Terry, at the time they bought a home. It stated specifically that the signers agreed to keep up the care of their lawns. Terry lived in a small Texas town.

   a. The police had the authority to issue a criminal citation to Terry for failing to live up to the agreement.
   b. The police had the authority to issue a criminal citation to Terry because he omitted to abide by a legal obligation that was specifically sanctioned by a local city ordinance that allowed homeowners' associations to require homeowners to engage in certain activities.
   c. Terry can be sued but there's no criminal matter here.
   d. Terry has a right not to cut his grass and live like nature intended.

8. As long as a defendant can produce some evidence that she did not intend to cause the harm that actually resulted from her actions, the trial court judge is obligated to give the jury an instruction on voluntariness.

    a. True
    b. False

9. Don was coming home from happy hour very tipsy when he noticed a person lying by the side of the road, obviously in pain. Don was a former medic in the armed services and decided to stop and see if the person needed assistance. Even in his drunken state, Don realized the person needed CPR, but he was tired and decided the heck with it. He didn't try to call out to other people who were passing by or make a 911 call on his cell phone. The person died. Doctors told police that if Don had performed CPR, the person probably would have lived.

    a. Don was cruel, but not guilty of a crime.
    b. The dead person's family can sue Don for being negligent, but that's all.
    c. Don assumed care of the person once he stopped to check on him and, therefore, is guilty.
    d. Don had the legal obligation to call for help if he did not intend to give it himself.

CHAPTER FOUR

THE GENERAL PRINCIPLES OF CRIMINAL LIABILITY: MENS REA, CONCURRENCE, CAUSATION

INTRODUCTION

This Chapter begins with a look at the difficult issue of criminal intent and ends with a discussion about strict liability and the causation requirement. With the important exceptions noted in Chapter Three, it is generally easy for a prosecutor to prove the actus reus of a crime. The greater challenge usually is to convince a judge or jury beyond a reasonable doubt that the defendant had the mens rea required by the statute under which he or she is being prosecuted. How do we reach into the hearts and minds of people to determine the whys and wherefores of their behavior? There may be no confession that clearly explains the defendant's mental state at the time the crime was committed. The defendant may choose not to testify. We rely on circumstantial evidence to help reveal criminal intent, such things as what crime occurred, what were the surrounding circumstances, how was the crime executed, and what victims and witnesses observed about the defendant's behavior and demeanor.

Criminal intent is one of the most complex areas of criminal law. The definitions of intent are necessarily vague and open-ended. The law recognizes that there are variations of intent because criminals are not equally blameworthy. Do we want to punish someone whose reckless driving caused a vehicular homicide the same way we punish someone who has committed a deliberate, cold-blooded murder? Is the bar room brawl that results in serious bodily harm the same crime as a carefully planned and executed assault that also causes serious injury?

CULPABLE MENTAL STATE

The State must prove the defendant's culpable mental state at the time of the offense beyond a reasonable doubt. Section 6.02 of the T.P.C. sets out the classification:

> (d) Culpable mental states are classified according to relative degrees, from highest to lowest, as follows:
> (1) intentional
> (2) knowing
> (3) reckless
> (4) criminal negligence

Section 6.03 defines those culpable mental states as:

(a) A person acts intentionally, or with intent, with respect to the nature of his conduct or to a result of his conduct when it is his conscious objective or desire to engage in the conduct or cause the result.
(b) A person acts knowingly, or with knowledge, with respect to the nature of his conduct or to the circumstances surrounding his conduct when he is aware of the nature of his conduct or that the circumstances exist. A person acts knowingly, or with knowledge, with respect to the result of his conduct when is he is aware that his conduct is reasonably certain to cause the result.
(c) A person acts recklessly, or is reckless, with respect to circumstances surrounding his conduct or the result of his conduct when he is aware of but consciously disregards a substantial and unjustifiable risk that the circumstances exist or the result will occur. The risk must be of such a nature and degree that its disregard constitutes a gross deviation from the standard of care that an ordinary person would exercise under all the circumstances as viewed from the actor's standpoint.
(d) A person acts with criminal negligence, or is criminally negligent, with respect to circumstances surrounding his conduct or the result of his conduct when he ought to be aware of a substantial and unjustifiable risk that the circumstances exist or the result will occur. The risk must be of such a nature and degree that the failure to perceive it constitutes a gross deviation from the standard of care that an ordinary person would exercise under all the circumstances as viewed from the actor's standpoint.

An accused's mental state can be inferred from his or her acts, words, and conduct. In determining culpability, the jury is entitled to consider events that occurred before, during, and after the commission of the crime.

When appellate courts review whether the evidence was sufficient, they must view the evidence in the light most favorable to the jury's verdict. Appellate courts are not in the business of setting aside jury verdicts. Their inquiry is whether any rational trier of fact would have found that the essential elements of the offense existed beyond a reasonable doubt. It is the jury's job to reconcile conflicting evidence and to judge the credibility of the witnesses.

Cases Interpreting Culpable Mental States

In *Norris v. State*, 902 S.W.2d 428 (Tex. Crim. App. 1995), the appellant was convicted of capital murder for killing his girlfriend and her two-year old child. He was angry with his girlfriend, went to her home with a high-powered deer rifle, and shot the baby and the mother at close range. Norris testified that he only intended to kill his girlfriend, but his girlfriend was holding the child when he aimed at her. In two statements made to the police after the crime, appellant never claimed that he accidentally killed the child. The jury was instructed that they could convict Norris of capital murder if they found he intentionally caused the death of the baby and the baby's mother and the deaths occurred during the same criminal transaction. Under the Penal Code, a person commits capital murder if he or she murders more than one person during the same criminal transaction.

The jury was also instructed that if Norris meant to cause the mother's death but accidentally caused the baby's death, the intent to kill the mother could be transferred to the baby. Under section 6.04(b) of the T.P.C., a person is criminally responsible for causing a result if the only difference between what actually happened and what he wanted to happen is that a different person was injured. Norris argued that there was insufficient evidence that he intended to kill the baby. The Criminal Court of Appeals disagreed and found that the close shooting and his failure to mention his lack of intent in statements to the police could lead a rational jury to find intent. The appellant also argued that the transfer doctrine should not be applied to capital murder prosecutions. By applying that doctrine, his homicides could be prosecuted as capital murders. The Court again disagreed, and Norris's murders were elevated to capital offenses.

The definitions of intentionally and knowingly performing an act were the focus of the court of appeals in the case *Hull v. State*, 871 S.W.2d 786, 787-789 (Tex. App. - Houston [14th Dist.] 1994). Hull was found guilty of murder. Read some of the court's opinion:

> The record reveals that on October 17, 1990, Tarra Smotherman and Terri Cross went to Pac's Ice House, located on Corpus Christi and Freeport Streets in Harris County, Texas. They visited with their friend Shorty, who introduced them to David Nash.
>
> Around 6:30 p.m., Jennifer Cater and her mother arrived at Pac's and invited the other two girls to go with them to Taco Bell. After leaving Taco Bell, Cater's mother drove back to Pac's and dropped off Cater, Smotherman, and Cross. Then Nash, Shorty, and the three girls got into Nash's car to go for a ride.
>
> They drove around for about an hour, and then Smotherman asked Nash to drop her off at a trailer house on Hershey Street. Nash drove to the trailer, and Smotherman got out of the car in front of appellant's house. When Nash drove down the dead end street to turn around, he saw Smotherman running down the street and appellant walking behind her.
>
> Cater yelled, "Watch out. He's starting to pop caps." Nash thought this meant that appellant was about to start shooting. Nash saw appellant raise his arm and aim a gun at them. Then, Nash ducked down over his car's console and accelerated past appellant.
>
> Nash heard a gunshot, and Shorty yelled that Cater had been hit.
> Nash stopped his car at the first intersection. Nash and Cross got out of the car and looked at Cater in the back seat. Cross left to call 911, and Nash and Shorty took Cater to the hospital, where she was later pronounced dead.
>
> * * * * *
>
> Here, appellant took the stand during the guilt-innocence phase of the trial. He testified that he intentionally shot at the car that Cater was riding in. He stated that he was not aiming the gun at any particular person, but he was trying to hit the car. He stated further that he did not know where the bullet went when he shot the gun. However, appellant admitted that he was aware when he shot the gun of the possibility that someone could have been killed.

Appellant argued that there was insufficient evidence for the jury to conclude that he intentionally or knowingly caused the death of Cater. The appeals court upheld the jury's guilty verdict by ruling that the jury could convict of murder if it believed the appellant <u>knowingly</u>

caused Cater's death. The evidence supported such a conclusion because it established that the appellant was aware his act could result in someone's death. A murder conviction can rest on facts that show a dangerous act was performed with knowledge of its possible consequences.

Robert Ormsby appealed his involuntary manslaughter conviction involving an accident that occurred when he fell asleep at the wheel of his automobile. His car crossed over the center line and struck an oncoming car, killing the driver. There was also evidence that the appellant was intoxicated. Ormsby wanted the jury to be instructed on the law of criminal negligence, a less serious offense that involuntary manslaughter. The Court of Criminal Appeals in *Ormsby v. State*, 600 S.W.2d 782 (Tex. Crim. App. 1980) compared the definitions of the two offenses:

Involuntary manslaughter, T.P.C. section 19.05(a):
(a) A person commits an offense if he:
(1) recklessly causes the death of an individual; or
(2) by accident or mistake when operating a motor vehicle while intoxicated and, by reason of such intoxication, causes the death of an individual.

Criminal negligence, T.P.C. section 19.07(a):
A person commits an offense if he causes the death of an individual by criminal negligence.

The court then noted the difference between how "reckless" and "negligent" are defined in T.P.C. sections 6.03(c) and (d) and concluded there was evidence of criminal negligence. The facts showed the appellant was driving while in a state of exhaustion and had driven this particular road many times. Coupled with his admitting that he had drank about three beers on an empty stomach prior to driving the car, there was sufficient evidence of criminal negligence to warrant a jury instruction about negligence.

Exercise:
In *Axelrod v. State*, 764 S.W.2d 296 (Tex. App. - Houston [1st Dist.] 1988), the appellant was convicted of intentionally or knowingly contributing to the delinquency of a minor by allowing four young men to remain in a bar where intoxicating liquor was consumed. Axelrod defended himself by stating that he did not know how old the young men were, and there was insufficient evidence that he intentionally contributed to their delinquency. There was some evidence, however, that the appellant saw the boys enter the club. The boys looked much younger than the other club patrons. The appellant had ample opportunity to watch them during the time they were in the club. How do you think the Houston Court of Appeals analyzed the issue of culpability? Did the appellant act intentionally, knowingly, or recklessly?

THE CAUSATION REQUIREMENT

Section 6.04(a) of the Texas Penal Code provides:

A person is criminally responsible if the result would not have occurred but for his conduct, operating either alone or concurrently with another cause, unless the concurrent cause was clearly sufficient to produce the result and the conduct of the other is clearly insufficient.

Paul Nugent was convicted of involuntary manslaughter as a result of an automobile collision he had with Marcus Meza. Three passengers in the Meza auto were killed. The evidence showed that Nugent was speeding greatly in excess of the speed limit and was intoxicated at the time of the accident. There was also evidence, however, that Meza's driving contributed to the accident. The jury charge read in *Nugent v. State*, 749 S.W.2d 595, 597 (Tex. App. - Corpus Christi 1988):

> Now if you believe from the evidence beyond a reasonable doubt that on or about the 16th day of February 1986, in Nueces County, Texas, the defendant, Paul Nugent, did then and there by accident and mistake, and by reason of such intoxication, *cause* the death of Marcus Anthony Meza, Jr., you will find the defendant guilty of involuntary manslaughter. Unless you so find beyond a reasonable doubt, or if you have a reasonable doubt thereof, you will acquit the defendant.

Nugent argued on appeal that the charge did not instruct the jury sufficiently on the issue of causation. The appellate court agreed with Nugent by first noting that a defendant is entitled to an instruction on every issue raised by the evidence. The instruction cannot just be an abstract explanation of what the Penal Code requires. It must be applied to the facts of the particular case. In this case, the jury should have been instructed that if they found Meza's driving was clearly sufficient to cause the accident and Nugent's conduct clearly insufficient to cause the accident, they should acquit Nugent.

Concurrent causation was not an issue, decided the appellate court in *Mendoza v. State*, 840 S.W.2d 697 (Tex. App. - Corpus Christi 1992). In that case Adriana Mendoza was convicted of murder. She claimed there was evidence of a concurrent cause sufficient to cause death. A pathologist testified the autopsy showed there was a stab wound to the victim's left upper chest that damaged two large blood vessels. In the pathologist's opinion the victim's chances for survival would have been pretty good if he had been treated in time by a competent vascular surgeon. Mendoza contended that because the victim failed to receive adequate medical treatment, there was insufficient evidence that she committed murder. The court decided that a person cannot be convicted when the person's conduct, by itself, is clearly insufficient to have caused the harm. When the evidence shows a causal connection between the defendant's conduct and the death of the deceased, there is no causation issue. In this case the evidence showed a causal connection between Mendoza's conduct of stabbing the victim and the victim's death.

A different pathologist testified in *Hutcheson v. State*, 899 S.W.2d 39 (Tex. App. - Amarillo 1995), that either the gunshot wound inflicted on the victim by his estranged wife or the gun shot wound inflicted on the victim by the police would have sufficed to cause death. The victim and the appellant had been arguing. The appellant shot the victim just as the police arrived on the scene. In the confusion, a police officer thought his fellow officer was under fire and shot the victim. Both the appellant's and the officer's shots inflicted extensive damage. The Amarillo Court of Appeals ruled that the appellant should be considered the cause of the victim's death.

STRICT LIABILITY

Strict liability offenses are provided for in Penal Code sections 6.02(b) and (c):

(b) If the definition of an offense does not prescribe a culpable mental state, a culpable mental state is nevertheless required unless the definition plainly dispenses with any mental element.
(c) If the definition of an offense does not prescribe a culpable mental state, but one is nevertheless required under Subsection (b), intent, knowledge, or recklessness suffices to establish criminal responsibility.

Cases Involving Strict Liability

Several cases have established the strict liability nature of offenses related to driving an automobile. In *Owen v. State*, 525 S.W.2d 165 (Tex. Crim. App. 1975), the court concluded that the crime of driving while intoxicated is a strict liability offense. In *Clayton v. State*, 652 S.W.2d 810 (Tex. App. - Amarillo 1983), the court decided that driving a car with a suspended driver's license is a strict liability offense. Exceeding the speed limit does not require mens rea as decided in *Zulauf v. State*, 591 S.W.2d 869 (Tex. Crim. App. 1979).

The strict liability issue was less clear, however, in *Pollard v. State*, 687 S.W.2d 373 (Tex. App. - Dallas 1985). In that case Garland Pollard was found guilty of sleeping and dozing in a public place in violation of a Dallas city ordinance. He argued that the complaint against him should be dismissed because it failed to allege a culpable mental state. The appellate court agreed. The Texas Constitution provides that no city ordinance shall contain a provision that is inconsistent with the state constitution or the laws enacted by the state legislature. The Dallas ordinance provided that a person commits an offense if he sleeps or dozes in a street, alley, park, or other public place. There was no mention in the ordinance of a required mental state. Looking at section 6.02 (a) and (b), the court ruled that when the city ordinance was enforced against Pollard without the requirement of a culpable mental state, it was inconsistent with section 6.02. Section 6.02 (b) provides that unless the definition of the offense plainly dispenses with any mental element, a culpable mental state is required. Concluded the court's opinion on page 374, "Since, as a result, a culpable mental state was an element of the offense of sleeping in public, the failure to allege that element renders the complaint fundamentally defective."

FINAL COMMENTS ON THE MENS REA, CONCURRENCE, AND CAUSATION

The principles of criminal liability discussed in this chapter are among the most difficult principles of criminal law. How do you determine just what a defendant was thinking and feeling at the time he or she committed a crime? Different jurors can listen to the same testimony and reach vastly different conclusions about an accused's mens rea. Proof is generally circumstantial. Perhaps the strength of the criminal law is that we attempt to determine culpability at all.

MULTIPLE CHOICE QUESTIONS

1. A negligent criminal act is committed if the actor:

    a. ignored a substantial and unjustifiable risk of which he ought to have been aware.
    b. ignored a substantial and unjustifiable risk of which he was aware.
    c. knew he was negligent.
    d. intended to be negligent.

2. An intentional act is committed if he or she:

    a. deliberately committed the act.
    b. planned the act in advance.
    c. consciously engaged in the act.
    d. is aware that his conduct is reasonably certain to cause a particular result.

3. As provided in the Texas Penal Code, proof of a higher degree of culpability than that charged constitutes proof of the culpability charged.

    a. True
    b. False

4. Culpable mental states are ranked from the highest to the lowest in the Texas Penal Code.

    a. True
    b. False

5. Unless otherwise stated in the definition of the offense, a culpable mental state is required according to the Penal Code.

    a. True
    b. False

6. Strict liability crimes are not permitted according to the Texas Constitution.

    a. True
    b. False

7. The defense that a concurrent cause eliminated criminal responsibility for harm or damage is only successful if the concurrent cause:

    a. was serious enough to have contributed to at least ½ of the harm done.
    b. was clearly sufficient to have produced the harm.
    c. was clearly sufficient to have produced the harm even if the actor's conduct was also clearly sufficient.
    d. was clearly sufficient to have produced the harm and the actor's conduct was clearly insufficient.

8. In cases involving issues of concurrent causation, the court is willing to split the criminal responsibility in such a way that each cause shares the criminal blame.

    a. True
    b. False

9. Bob shot his gun in Mandy's direction, not to do bodily harm but to scare her. He did not intend for the bullet to strike. The wind, however, carried the bullet toward Gary, who made a sharp movement just as the bullet was speeding by. Gary was hit by Bob's bullet and killed. Bob is deeply grieved.

    a. Bob can argue that his bullet was never directed at Gary, so he's not guilty of a crime.
    b. Bob can argue that he never intended for anyone to be harmed, therefore, he is not guilty of a crime.
    c. Bob's in trouble. His actions were arguably criminally negligent.
    d. Bob killed someone and it does not matter what his mens rea was at the time.

10. Sara refused to testify at her murder trial. She never confessed to the murder. The only evidence the State has is an eyewitness who saw Sara take a loaded gun into a room and close the door. The witness then heard a loud bang and saw Sara rush out of the room and proceed out the building. The witness went into the room and found Skippy's dead body with a bullet in his chest. The gun that shot Skippy was never found. Sara had no gun residue on her hands when she was arrested.

    a. There is no direct evidence against Sara and the State cannot not prove her guilt beyond a reasonable doubt.
    b. If the witness is credible, the State has a case.
    c. There is no way for the State to prove up Sara's mens rea even if they could prove up her actus reus.
    d. The jury will be instructed to assume that Sara intentionally shot the victim.

CHAPTER FIVE

PARTIES TO CRIME:
COMPLICITY AND VICARIOUS LIABILITY

INTRODUCTION

> **Exercise:**
> Seven male prisoners escaped from a Texas maximum-security prison facility on November 13, 2000. While burglarizing an Oshman's Sporting Good Store in Irving, Texas on Christmas Eve, where they stole a cache of guns and ammunition, one of the now infamous "Texas Seven," George Rivas, shot and killed Aubry Hawkins, an Irving police officer. After evading law enforcement for over a month, five of the seven escapees were apprehended in Colorado on January 15, 2001. One of the five committed suicide rather than be arrested. Two days later the other two escapees were finally taken into custody, also apprehended in Colorado.
> All six prisoners have been charged with capital murder for killing Officer Hawkins during the commission of a felony. Several of the escapees say they plan to fight the charge on the grounds they did not shoot and never intended to commit the crime of murder. George Rivas has admitted that he shot and killed Officer Hawkins.
> How do you think the prosecution will argue the law of parties against the five prisoners who did not fire the shot at Officer Hawkins? How will their attorneys respond?

This chapter looks at the law of parties in Texas, sections 7.01 and 7.02 of the Penal Code. Like most states, Texas has abolished the common law distinctions between accomplices and principals. According to the T.P.C., each party to an offense may be charged and convicted of that offense.

COMPLICITY STATUTES: THE LAW OF PARTIES

Section 7.01 provides:

(a) A person is criminally responsible as a party to an offense if the offense is committed by his own conduct, by the conduct of another for which he is criminally responsible, or by both.
(b) Each party to an offense may be charged with commission of the offense.

A person is criminally responsible for an offense committed by the conduct of another if, according to section 7.02:

>(a)(1) acting with the kind of culpability required for the offense, he cause or aids an innocent or nonresponsible person to engage in conduct prohibited by the definition of the offense;
>(a)(2) acting with intent to promote or assist the commission of the offense, he solicits, encourages, directs, aids, or attempts to aid the other person to commit the offense; or
>(a)(3) having a legal duty to prevent commission of the offense and acting with intent to promote or assist its commission, he fails to make a reasonable effort to prevent commission of the offense.

According to the penal code, allegations that an accused was a party to an offense must be supported by sufficient evidence that the accused acted with the intent (mens rea) to promote or assist in the commission of the offense and solicited, encouraged, directed, aided, or attempted to aid (actus reus) a person to commit a crime.

Sufficiency of Evidence

By now you recognize how reluctant appellate courts are to overturn the decisions of trial courts. They are especially reluctant to overturn jury verdicts when a convicted offender alleges on appeal that there was insufficient evidence to convict him. It's one thing to overturn a case because there was a violation of an accused's Fourth Amendment search and seizure right or Sixth Amendment right to counsel. It's another thing altogether for an appellate court to sit in judgment on the facts of a case. In Texas, as in every jurisdiction, courts of appeal have held that evidence will be considered sufficient to support a conviction if after the court evaluates the evidence <u>in the light most favorable to the verdict</u>, it concludes that a rational jury would have found the elements of the offense beyond a reasonable doubt. The jury members are the factfinders. It is their exclusive right to decide the credibility, weight, and balance of the evidence. An appellate court steps in only when a jury's decision is so against the great weight and preponderance of the evidence as to be manifestly unjust.

Cases involving the law of parties are often based on circumstantial evidence as opposed to direct evidence. Direct evidence would include a confession or eyewitness testimony about what actually occurred. It is evidence that directly demonstrates the ultimate fact to be proved. Circumstantial evidence is direct proof of a secondary fact that logically demonstrates the ultimate fact to be proved. In a circumstantial evidence case, proof amounting to a strong suspicion is not enough to support a conviction. However, every fact in a case need not point directly and independently to the defendant's guilt. A guilty verdict can rest on the combined and cumulative force of all the incriminating circumstances.

As you read about the Texas cases in this chapter and throughout the Supplement, notice how difficult it is for an appellant to convince an appeals court to reverse his or her case based on the theory that there was insufficient evidence proving they were parties to criminal activity.

Cases Interpreting the Law of Parties

Often the facts are clear that the appellant was a party to the crime. Wilkerson drove the getaway car in the aggravated robbery of a convenience store. The appellate court in *Wilkerson v. State*, 874 S.W.2d 127 (Tex. App. - Houston [14th Dist.] 1994), had no problem in finding that the facts supported the jury's decision that he was a party to the robbery. The fact that he did not personally enter the store during the robbery was irrelevant because there was sufficient evidence that he cooperated and aided in the commission of the crime.

A similar conclusion was reached in *Gilchrest v. State*, 904 S.W.2d 935 (Tex. App. - Amarillo 1995). Gilchrest was also convicted of aggravated robbery. Gilchrest was driving a pick-up truck around town with a friend in the passenger seat. They found an elderly woman on foot to rob. The passenger reached over and grabbed her purse. Gilchrest accelerated the truck, and the passenger pulled the purse off the victim's arm. The fact that Gilchrest did not grab the purse himself did not change the other facts in evidence that he had aided and abetted the robbery.

In *McCraw v. State*, 690 S.W.2d 69 (Tex. App. - Dallas 1985), the McGraw was found guilty of participating in a burglary to a habitation even though he never entered the home. He did, however, receive stolen property through the window of the home as it was being burgled, and he warned a neighbor not to call the police. The court concluded there was sufficient evidence that McCraw was a party to the crime. The law of parties is a very important mechanism by which the State can charge and convict people like Wilkerson, Gilchrest, and McCraw.

Hill v. State

Sometimes the facts are complex. Read excerpts from the case *Hill v. State*, 883 S.W.2d 765, 767-768 (Tex. App. – Amarillo 1994) and determine whether there was sufficient evidence of both mens rea and actus reus to convict Anita Mae Hill of injury to a child.

> Jason Hill, the nine year old son of appellant and her husband, Marvin Hill, was admitted to Northwest Texas Hospital on 17 May 1990 with severe and infected bruises and injuries, admittedly inflicted by his father in "spanking" him with a metal rod. Carolyn Jordan, a registered nurse, noticed Jason had various bruises and injuries obviously inflicted at different times, some of which were emitting a greenish pus with blackened, dead skin over or around them. The injuries were the worst she had ever seen, and were of a type causing permanent disfigurement.
>
> * * * * *
>
> Marvin confessed to Corporal Michael Allen, an Amarillo police officer, that several days before, he had taken a metal rod from a screen door, located at his home, and spanked Jason. Although he spanked Jason repeatedly, Marvin said he did not realize he had injured him badly.

* * * * *

Jason testified that for several years before the event leading to the prosecution, Marvin, and sometimes appellant herself, would beat him with a metal rod or stick. Jennifer and Heidi [Jason's sisters], who had been beaten by Marvin in their parents' bedroom, confirmed Jason's beatings by his father, and Jennifer said that when appellant asked Marvin not to do those things, he would become abusive toward her. Usually, Jason said, appellant would report to Marvin that he had been bad, and Marvin would beat him.

* * * * *

The testimony of Karlene Conner, the Hill's former next door neighbor, was that Jason acted scared all the time, and he would recoil from her anytime she made a movement toward him. On six or seven occasions when Marvin was not home, she would hear the children screaming, "no, Mommy, no," for periods of at least one hour. Her daughter, Leslie Conner, said the family stopped using their backyard swimming pool because they got tired of hearing the Hill children crying all day and screaming, "No, mommie. Please mommie, stop."

* * * * *

Kim Wrazidlo, the Texas Department of Protective and Regulatory Services caseworker who accompanied the officers to the Hill residence, said appellant was concerned with what was happening to Marvin, and did not inquire about Jason.

* * * * *

After the emergency hearing requested by the Department to remove the Hill children to a foster home, Rick Keffler, an attorney who represented appellant at the hearing, drove Marvin to the hospital. He recalled that Marvin said he alone had caused the injuries to Jason and that appellant did not have anything to do with it.

* * * * *

Appellant's friend, Nadine Boyd, who knew the Hills since 1985 and often visited in their home, testified that when she was with appellant and the children in the absence of Marvin, there was no violence and the children acted normal, but when Marvin was present, the children were very subdued and quiet. She never saw injuries on the children.

Jan Markham, who lived with the Hills for two months in 1988 and saw appellant daily until she moved away, stated it was a very pleasant atmosphere, the children were not afraid of appellant, and showed her great affection. Marvin was extremely strict, the children appeared to be fearful of him, and he was cruel to them.
Pat Walsh generally confirmed the testimony of his wife, Betty Walsh, Boyd and Markham. He stated the children were quiet, that appellant was a very solicitous mother, and that he saw no signs of physical abuse on the children.

Given this evidence, appellant presents two challenges to its sufficiency to support her conviction. Initially, she points out that to convict her under the law of parties, the State had to prove conduct by Marvin that constituted an offense, plus conduct by her with the intent to promote or assist Marvin's conduct.

* * * * *

Appellant contends that the evidence does not show any act on her part which promoted or assisted Marvin in the commission of the offense, but if there is, then there is absolutely no evidence of her intent to promote or assist the commission of the offense of causing serious bodily injury to Jason.

* * * * *

Appellant acknowledges that in determining whether an individual is a party to an offense and bears criminal responsibility, the court may look to events before, during, and after the commission of the offense. Circumstantial evidence may be sufficient to show that an individual is a party to the offense, and it is not necessary that the individual be present at the scene of the crime. *Morrison v. State*, 608 S.W.2d 233, 234 (Tex. Crim. App. 1980).

From the evidence, the jury could discern a pattern, existing during a number of years, that on the occasions when Marvin arrived home from work and appellant told him one of the children had been bad, Marvin would take the child into his bedroom and "spank" the child with a metal rod or a stick. There was evidence that these "spankings" had resulted in physical injuries to the children, including knots on the heads of Jennifer and Heidi, and the fracture of eight of Jason's ribs. On some of these occasions, appellant would be present; at other times she would leave the house at Marvin's direction. The jury could reasonably infer from the evidential pattern that on the last occasion when Marvin arrived at home and engaged in a conversation with appellant, followed by Marvin's immediate beating of Jason, appellant had told Marvin Jason had been bad, knowing that Marvin would "spank" him. Thus, the evidence is sufficient for the jury to find that appellant, albeit not present during the "spanking" acted to promote or assist in the "spanking" of Jason.

After examining the actus reus element of the charge against the appellant, the court examined the mens rea element.

Nevertheless, appellant proposes, without disagreement by the State, that to be criminally responsible, the evidence must show not only that she acted to promote or assist in Jason's "spanking," but that she intended to promote or assist the commission of the offense of causing serious bodily injury to a child. ... It follows that appellant is criminally responsible for the offense committed by Marvin only if the evidence shows that she *knew Marvin's unlawful intent* when she acted to promote or assist in his conduct.

The evidence heard by the jury included testimony bearing on appellant's knowledge of Marvin's unlawful intent. ... Consequently, the evidence, viewed in the light most favorable to the verdict, is sufficient for any rational trier of fact to have found appellant criminally responsible for the offense committed by Marvin beyond a reasonable doubt. Her point of error is overruled.

The judgment is affirmed.

Anita Mae Hill was found guilty of the same offense as Marvin Hill even though there was no evidence that she administered the "spanking" in question or that she was even present when it occurred. The jury could infer from her actions that she promoted or assisted in the "spankings" (her actus reus) and intended to promote the causing of serious bodily harm to a child (her mens rea).

Present at the Crime Scene v. Party to a Crime

Mere physical presence at a crime scene is not enough evidence of complicity. Alfonso Urtado was convicted of attempted burglary of a habitation in the case *Urtado v. State*, 605 S.W.2d 907 (Tex. Crim. App. 1980). Like Anita Mae Hill, he alleged in his appeal that there was insufficient evidence that he aided and abetted the commission of a crime. Tom DeLoach testified that he observed a strange man and two women in a neighbor's back yard. He saw the man making a cutting-type motion across the top of the neighbor's kitchen window while the two women stood and watched. That man was later identified as Urtado. DeLoach did not observe a tool or object in the Urtado's hand. DeLoach approached the man and the women and asked if they were trying to break in the house. The three left quickly, got into the same car and sped away. The evidence showed that there was a ten to twelve inch cut across the top rim of the window screen.

Urtado's testimony was that he drove the two young women to apply for jobs as housekeepers for a home advertised in the newspaper. He and the young women testified that they had difficulty locating the right house. The girls told Urtado to wait in the car for them while they walked down the street. They knocked on the door of the almost burglarized home. When no one answered, the girls walked around to the back door, took out a knife and started to cut the window screen. Urtado appeared, scolded the young women, examined the damage to the screen, and told them they were leaving. As they were exiting the yard, they met up with DeLoach. Concerned and afraid, all three walked quickly to the car and left the scene as fast as they could. The women testified that their decision to burglarize the house was made on the spur of the moment and that Urtado was not aware of their actions until he caught them in the act.

The Court of Appeals emphasized that to be guilty of a crime requires more than physical presence. Appellant's "flight" from the scene and his assistance in helping the young women leave did not amount to an agreement to commit a burglary. In this case, the appellate court concluded that the evidence presented at trial was insufficient for a conviction. Aiding and abetting a crime requires more than Urtado's actions.

> **Exercises:**
>
> In *Williams v. State*, 760 S.W.2d 292 (Tex. App. - Texarkana 1988), Williams was found guilty of burglarizing a motor vehicle. The facts showed that Williams and his friend House were together on July 30, 1987. A police officer caught House breaking into a car. He pled guilty and stated that Williams did not know that he was planning a break-in. Williams testified that he was with House prior to the break-in but denied any involvement. A police officer testified that he and his partner followed Williams and House for several miles through parking lots and watched them crisscross from one car to another looking into the cars. Williams stopped at the rear of the burgled car, constantly looking up and down the street and sidewalks while House broke in. The officers arrested them both. Williams gave a false name and carried a pair of vise grip pliers commonly used by car thieves. Did Williams win his challenge to the sufficiency of the evidence?
> Detail the arguments for and against his case.
>
> Read the case *Lacy v. State*, 782 S.W.2d 556 (Tex. App. - Houston [14th Dist.] 1989). Lacy was convicted of delivery of a controlled substance, crack cocaine. He argued in his appeal that there was insufficient evidence of his guilt under the law of parties. Undercover narcotics officers approached the appellant Lacy at a strip shopping center in Houston, Texas. After a short conversation, an unsuspecting Lacy led the officers to an apartment complex where the officers completed a drug transaction with an unknown third person. The unknown person delivered the cocaine to the officers and took their money. Lacy requested a sample of the cocaine from the officers, but he did not deliver the drugs to them nor did he receive money from them. Lacy was arrested and convicted of delivery of a controlled substance. Appellant relied on a decision of the Texas Court of Criminal Appeals in *Conaway v. State*, 738 S.W.2d 692 (Tex. Crim. App. 1987), which held that delivery of a controlled substance may be accomplished through actual transfer, constructive transfer, or offer to sell. The State argued in the *Lacy* case that Lacy had actually transferred the drugs to the officers. According to the *Conaway* decision, however, actual delivery requires a complete transfer of real possession and control of a drug from one person to another. Surrounding circumstances and participation in negotiations cannot convert what could be construed as constructive delivery to actual delivery. Lacy claimed that the State could not make a case of actual delivery against him. The difference between the *Lacy* and *Conaway* decisions was that in *Lacy* the State had argued the law of parties. In *Conaway*, the State had not argued the law of parties. How do you think the law of parties affected the appellate court's ruling in the *Lacy* case? Did the law of parties help the State's conviction of Lacy on a delivery charge?
>
> See another case with very similar facts: *Francis v. State*, 909 S.W.2d 158 (Tex. App. - Houston [14th Dist.] 1995).

In *Guillory v. State*, 877 S.W.2d 71 (Tex. App. - Houston [1st Dist.] 1994), the appellant was convicted of being a party to a robbery. He admitted he was more than just present at the scene of the crime but argued that he was only guilty of helping the robber avoid capture. Betty Howard was in a Kroger parking lot when Jamie McBride grabbed her arm, threw her against the car, took her purse, and ran off. Guillory drove a late model pick-up truck by McBride and opened the passenger door. McBride jumped in, and the truck drove away. Onlookers tried to stop the truck. Several hours later, McBride and Guillory returned to the store in a different vehicle. The security guard recognized them and called the police. Several people identified them as the robbers, and they were arrested.

Guillory alleged at most the facts showed he assisted McBride in avoiding capture. It was certainly in Guillory's best interest to argue that he assisted in McBride's escape. Section 38.05 of the Texas Penal Code addresses Hindering Apprehension or Prosecution. Robbery is a second-degree felony. Hindering apprehension is a third-degree felony. The appeals court, however, upheld the jury's verdict. Although there were no facts in evidence as to what the truck was doing before the robbery or whether McBride and Guillory were seen together at the parking lot before the crime, there was evidence that Guillory drove the truck very quickly, picked up McBride after the robbery, and opened the passenger door for her to get in. There was evidence that when the two were finally arrested, they possessed items they had shoplifted from the store and that they were romantically involved. This was clearly a case of circumstantial evidence, which the appellate court considered persuasive enough for a jury to infer that Guillory was a party to robbery.

A very serious issue involving the law of parties was raised *In the Matter of D.L.N.*, 930 S.W.2d 253, 256 (Tex. App. - Houston [14th Dist.] 1996). D.L.N. was a juvenile charged with capital murder. He was transferred from the juvenile system to the adult system for trial as an adult. His appeal came up in the context of his certification proceeding. He alleged there was insufficient evidence to support a probable cause finding that he was a party to a murder and should be transferred to the adult justice system.

The facts showed that D.L.N. and his friend Gartrell had been discussing the possibility of committing a car-jacking. D.L.N. followed Gartrell's instructions to take a gun from the bedroom of a father of one of their friends. At Gartrell's house, the two of them took turns firing the pistol into the air. They also drank several bottles of beer and became "pretty drunk." A friend took them to a store parking lot. They switched off carrying the gun in their pants. Gartrell told D.L.N., "let's just carjack that fool right there," as a Mustang drove by, and D.L.N. said, "shut up, don't be stupid." They walked over to the store and bought cigarettes. The court opinion reads:

> Gartrell saw a truck he wanted to carjack, and appellant said, "alright dude, whatever." Appellant heard a gunshot, which killed Joe Darin Campbell, and then saw Gartrell drive around some apartments and pull up to where he was. Gartrell told appellant, "get in." Appellant ran around to the passenger's side, got into the truck, and they drove off.
>
> Later, appellant helped dispose of the truck by putting it into neutral to roll into a creek. Appellant took off his socks so he could wipe down the truck and the gun clip. In addition, appellant discarded the gun Gartrell used to kill Campbell.
>
> [Police Officer Shirley Brown] testified that there was no evidence that appellant shot Joe Darin Campbell.

The appeals court ruled there was enough evidence that D.L.N. was not merely present at the crime scene and to find there was probable cause that he was a party to the commission of a capital murder, the same offense charged against Gartrel. The law of parties opened the door to an adult criminal conviction for capital murder even though D.L.N. was not the shooter, and there was some evidence that he was not present at the murder itself.

> **Exercise:**
> Texas courts recognize the "independent impulse" defense to a charge under the law of parties, *Fincher v. State*, 980 S.W.2d 886 (Tex. App.- Fort Worth 1998). Under this theory, the accused admits that although he intended to break the law, he did not contemplate the extent of wrongdoing that his fellow conspirators actually engaged in. For this reason he should not be held criminally responsible for their conduct. The courts are careful, however, to apply this defense very narrowly. The defense is not available if the crime was committed to further the unlawful purpose in which all the conspirators were involved, <u>and</u> it was a crime the accused should have anticipated might happen as a result of committing the offense they had agreed to. How could this defense be argued when D.L.N. faces his capital murder trial? Or the Texas prison escapees discussed at the beginning of this chapter?

FINAL COMMENTS ON THE LAW OF PARTIES

The law of parties aims to enlarge the criminal justice net to include individuals who should be held criminally liable for actions they may not have caused directly but in which they exercised some significant level of participation. The difficult issue becomes at what point do we want to wield the power of the State against a person who aided, encouraged or abetted the commission of a crime. At what point should moral culpability be considered legal culpability? When did Anita Mae Hill's failure to act become criminal? At what point did D.L.N.'s admittedly culpable behavior become serious enough to result in a charge of capital murder? Why is it good public policy to hold someone liable for an offense he should have anticipated that his criminal co-conspirator would commit? The complicity statutes are important because they allow the prosecution of persons who could otherwise hide behind the fact that they themselves were not the shooter or the abuser. On the other hand, the law of parties should not be permitted to reach too far. At some point, the criminal justice system is not the appropriate vehicle of social control.

MULTIPLE CHOICE QUESTIONS

1. The phrase "law of parties" refers to:

    a. the laws that define what types of parties involve criminal nuisance.
    b. the laws that relate to complicity and participation in criminal offenses.
    c. the manner in which the government decides the amount of punishment that should be administered to various convicted defendants involved in the same criminal transaction.
    d. how responsibility is assigned to the various individuals involved in a crime depending on whether they were at the scene of the crime or not.

2. Ben decided to rob a convenience store on his way home from work. The only problem was his younger brother Teddy was with him, and Teddy was studying for the priesthood. Ben robbed the store clerk while Teddy was a few feet away looking longingly at the candy bars. Teddy was shocked by what he saw and heard but was caught up in the moment. As Ben ran out the door, Teddy ran after him. The police caught them both a few blocks from the store.

    a. Teddy can be convicted as a party to the robbery because he is Ben's brother and was at the scene of the crime.
    b. Teddy can be convicted as a party to the robbery because he fled with Ben.
    c. Teddy cannot be convicted of robbery unless there is evidence that shows he gave assistance to the crime.
    d. Teddy cannot be convicted of robbery because there is no evidence that he demanded money from the clerk.

3. The surrounding circumstances and events before and after the commission of a crime can be introduced into evidence to support a finding that a defendant was a party to a crime.

    a. True
    b. False

4. A conviction based on the law of parties must have some direct evidence as its basis.

    a. True
    b. False

5. The law of parties only requires a finding that the defendant assisted or aided in the commission of the crime. It does not require separate proof that the defendant intended to aid in the commission of a crime.

    a. True
    b. False

6. Helen studied section 7.02 of the Texas Penal Code. She noticed that if she encouraged her husband to bribe a public official, she could face charges of being a party to his crime. Helen decided she would not voice any encouragement, but neither would she advise him not to engage in bribery when he discussed it with her (they discuss all their business with each other):

    a. Helen could still face charges under the law of parties for her failure to advise her husband that bribery is against the law.
    b. Helen could still face charges because she knew what her husband was contemplating and failed to inform the authorities.
    c. Helen probably will not face charges because there will be no evidence that she encouraged her husband to break the law.
    d. Helen could still face charges because by her silence she gave tacit encouragement.

7. The best lesson a person can learn after reading about the law of parties:

    a. Beware who your friends are.
    b. Beware who your friends are and what activities you engage in with them.
    c. Don't agree to pick up a friend from a bank or convenience store. Tell them to take a taxi.
    d. Be careful not to put agreements in writing.

8. According to the Texas Penal Code, if the person who committed an offense is acquitted, the person who is being prosecuted as a party to that same offense cannot be convicted.

    a. True
    b. False

9. According to the Texas Penal Code, if the person who committed an offense is found guilty of a certain type or class of crime, the person who has been charged as a party to that same offense can only be convicted of that same crime.

    a. True
    b. False

10. The law of parties requires all persons to attempt to stop crimes from being committed in their presence because that is our legal duty as citizens.

    a. True, see T.P.C. section 7.01
    b. True, see T.P.C. section 7.02(a)(3)
    c. False, see T.P.C. section 7.01(a)(3)
    d. False, see the Texas Constitution

CHAPTER SIX

UNCOMPLETED CRIMES: ATTEMPT, CONSPIRACY, AND SOLICITATION

INTRODUCTION

This chapter looks at the law of attempt, conspiracy and solicitation in Texas. As you read the cases, ask yourself how you would argue as a prosecutor to sustain a conviction on appeal and then as a defense attorney attempting to overturn your client's conviction. Many cases on appeal involve very close judgment calls. The facts are often subject to interpretation and manipulation. Criminal attempt and conspiracy statutes are especially subject to debate. Being able to argue both sides of a legal issue may seem awkward at first. You may have a sense about what you think is a correct result and be reluctant to champion the opposite position. The more you take time to understand the other side, however, to the point where you can be its advocate, your understanding of the law will increase considerably. You will better understand the statute, what criminal behavior it is intended to prohibit or deter, and what type of offender should be brought into the criminal justice system with all its awesome power. The best advocates know and appreciate their opponents' arguments.

ATTEMPTING TO COMMIT A CRIME

Section 15.01 of the Texas Penal Code provides:

(a) A person commits an offense if, with specific intent to commit an offense, he does an act amounting to more than mere preparation that tends but fails to effect the commission of the offense intended.

* * * * *

(c) It is no defense to prosecution for criminal attempt that the offense attempted was not actually committed.

The two elements of criminal attempt law that generate most appeals are the mens rea requirement of "specific intent to commit an offense" and the actus reus requirement of performing an act that amounts to "more than mere preparation." In the Texas cases discussed in this chapter, the appellants often challenge their conviction on the grounds there was insufficient evidence to prove both the actus reus and mens rea of attempt beyond a reasonable doubt. Most appeals are a combination of several different legal challenges. From an appellant's perspective, every reasonable legal argument should be made as long as it falls within a State's requirements to appeal. In addition, defense attorneys are obligated by their professional code of ethics to represent their clients zealously.

As you read the cases presented in this chapter, notice how the appellants' lawyers weave the stories about the crimes their clients were convicted of around the legal requirements of the statutes. Stories about greed, hate, love, obsession, and fear are reinterpreted in the light of legal doctrines that, in the case of criminal attempt law, impose concepts like "specific intent" and beyond "mere preparation" in a way that sometimes strain the actual events. The ability to weave facts creatively and persuasively around legal definitions is the skill of lawyering.

Cases Interpreting the Law of Attempt

Acts Beyond Mere Preparation

Three of the cases in this section discuss the crime of attempted burglary. After reading the about the cases, can you see why a defense attorney would challenge allegations of attempted burglary on the basis that there was insufficient evidence of an act amounting to more than mere preparation?

The T.P.C. section 30.04 defines burglary of a vehicle:

(a) A person commits an offense if, without the effective consent of the owner, he breaks into or enters a vehicle or any part of a vehicle with intent to commit a felony or theft.
(b) For purposes of this section, 'enter' means to intrude:
(1) any part of the body; or
(2) any physical object connected with the body

Attempted burglary of a vehicle was charged in *Bledsoe v. State*, 578 S.W.2d 123, 125 (Tex. Crim. App. 1979). In that case, a Dallas police officer was called to the scene of an attempted burglary and found Bledsoe near the passenger side door of a 1979 Ford L.T.D. He observed Bledsoe duck between the cars as if he was trying to conceal himself. The officer searched the immediate area and found a screwdriver and a clothes hanger on the ground approximately three feet from Bledsoe. The officer arrested him. The officer testified at Bledsoe's trial that he could not see the appellant's hands because he was facing away from him and could only guess that Bledsoe was trying to unlock the car door. There was no evidence of scratches or marks on the L.T.D.

Assuming for the moment that the appellant was burglarizing a car, did his activity amount to more than mere preparation? He was not seen touching the car. He was not on the parking lot premises unlawfully. And how important is the screwdriver and clothes hanger? The Texas Court of Criminal Appeals stated, "Nor, under the circumstances, do we attach significance to the fact that a screwdriver and clothes hanger were found within the appellant's immediate control. A person should not be held criminally responsible simply because a vigilant police officer intervenes before he begins to implement his criminal designs." The court set aside Bledsoe's conviction. Notice the court does not suggest the appellant was innocent. The opinion noted that if the police officer had arrived on the scene a few minutes (seconds?) later,

Bledsoe may have gone beyond mere preparation and entered the realm of criminal attempt. There was a vigorous dissenting opinion that said the facts supported an attempted criminal act. How close was the call in your mind?

The Texas Court of Criminal Appeals also decided *Flournoy v. State*, 668 S.W.2d 380 (Tex. Crim. App. 1984) which involved an attempted burglary of a habitation. Lyndia Conley was in her mobile home at approximately 9:00 a.m. when she observed Mr. Flournoy accompanied by a passenger, park a car, get out, and approach her house. The passenger remained in the car. Conley did not recognize Flournoy or the passenger. She checked her front and back doors and placed herself in a position to watch what was going on outside. Flournoy knocked on the front door. When no one responded, the passenger got out of the car and went to the rear of the mobile home where he tried to look in the windows, but they were too high for him to see in so he returned to the car. Conley testified at trial that Flournoy tried to unlock the front door with a screwdriver or some other tool. He tried to get through the screen door to the main door. At this point, Conley got her rifle, opened the front door and told Flournoy to leave. He ran to the car and sped away. Conley made a note of the license plate number and called the police who arrested Flournoy for attempted burglary.

The intermediate court of appeals ruled there was insufficient evidence of attempted burglary because Flournoy's acts did not go beyond mere preparation. They were concerned that the only evidence was Conley's interpretation of what she thought the appellant was trying to do. The higher court disagreed and found that when Flournoy reached his hand through Conley's screen door, his act amounted to more than mere preparation. Appellate courts are obligated to review the evidence in the light most favorable to the jury's verdict. In this case, the Court of Criminal Appeals concluded that Conley's own observations of the appellant's behavior provided sufficient evidence to support the jury's findings, and a rational trier of fact could conclude that Flournoy was attempting a burglary.

Another problematic attempted burglary case is *Molenda v. State*, 712 S.W.2d 525 (Tex. App. - Beaumont 1984). Molenda was convicted of the attempted burglary of a building, which was located in the middle of a 500-acre tract of land, the entire acreage surrounded by a fence. The facts showed that Molenda pried off the lock on the fence and entered the 500-acre premises. He was convicted of attempting to burglarize the building. The court of appeals ruled that at the most Molenda could be found guilty of criminal mischief, injury to the fence, or criminal trespass.

Exercise:
Proving beyond a reasonable doubt that a defendant performed acts beyond mere preparation makes attempt law a very tricky endeavor. By its very nature, burglary involves sneaky, undercover activities that can be interpreted in different ways. It is not an easy task for the prosecutor to take those actions and weave the story that they cross the line that separates preparation from actually effecting the crime. In the *Bledsoe, Flournoy,* and *Molenda* cases, the courts relied on shades of differences in the circumstances surrounding the charges even though the facts strongly suggested that all three appellants were up to no good. How do these three cases differ? How do those differences affect the courts' different decisions?

Attempted arson was the conviction in *Cody v. State*, 605 S.W.2d 271,273 (Tex. Crim. App. 1980). Officer Silva observed Cody pouring a substance on the floor of a school building. Silva determined that the substance was gasoline and that several wads of paper had been placed on the floor near the gasoline. Silva placed Cody under arrest and found matches in his pockets. Following his arrest, Cody admitted in a written statement that he intended to set the school building on fire. In his appeal, he argued, however, that because he never struck a match, the evidence of attempted arson was insufficient to convict him. The Court of Criminal Appeals responded, "This argument is based on the mistaken premise that the attempt statute requires that *every* act short of actual commission be accomplished in order for one to be convicted of an attempted offense. The statute only requires an act tending to effect the commission of the offense." In this case, the court concluded that Cody performed such an act and sustained his conviction.

Domitillo Moreno was convicted of the attempted aggravated sexual assault of his eleven-year-old niece in *Moreno v. State*, 872 S.W.2d 1 (Tex. App. – Houston [1st Dist.] 1993). The victim testified that Moreno told her to take off her clothes because he wanted to have sex with her. When she refused, he slapped her face, punched the wall of the room, and threatened to punch her. When she tried to get away, he pushed her on the bed and stuffed a rag in her mouth. She was able to remove the rag and scream for help. The appellant left, and the girl ran out of the house. The Texas Penal Code defines aggravated sexual assault of a child in section 22.021 and requires certain specific acts: penetration of a female sex organ or anus, penetration of the mouth of the victim with a sex organ, causing the sex organ of a victim to contact or penetrate the mouth, anus, or sex organ of a perpetrator. Moreno did not pretend that he was an innocent man. He argued there was not enough evidence that he attempted to perform the actions required under the sexual assault statute. The Court of Appeals sustained Moreno's conviction. "There was no fondling or touching of the victim, but the appellant threatened her, punched the wall, pushed her on the bed and put a rag in her mouth. The fact that the appellant left before completing the act does not negate his intent."

Exercises:

Jack Baxter was convicted of attempted aggravated manufacture of methamphetamine. During a search of Baxter's home, police found many of the chemicals and much of the equipment to manufacture methamphetamine, however, they did not find one ingredient essential – methylamine. Baxter argued that without finding methylamine, there was insufficient evidence to convict him of attempted manufacture. How do you think the court ruled in *Baxter v. State*, 718 S.W.2d 28 (Tex. App. – Eastland 1986)?

Gerry Giddings was convicted of attempted possession of cocaine in an amount of 400 grams or more. He attacked the sufficiency of evidence based on an argument of factual impossibility. He was arrested immediately after two undercover police officers negotiated a deal to "sell" him the cocaine. Giddings argued that because the officers did not have the cocaine to sell it was factually impossible for him to attempt to possess it. What do you think the court concluded? Did Giddings' acts amount to more than mere preparation? See *Giddings v. State*, 816 S.W.2d 538 (Tex. App. - Dallas 1991).

Section 19.03 of the Texas Penal Code, discussed in Chapter 8, outlines the offense of capital murder. Section 19.03(a)(2) is the felony-murder statute and provides that a person commits a capital murder if:

> the person intentionally commits the murder in the course of committing or attempting to commit kidnapping, burglary, robbery, aggravated sexual assault, arson, or obstruction or retaliation.

The State had to prove the crime attempted kidnapping beyond a reasonable doubt in the case *Santellan v. State*, 939 S.W.2d 155 (Tex. Crim. App. 1997), in order to convict the appellant of capital murder. Santellan and his girlfriend were having relationship problems. After writing a letter addressed to his family apologizing for the murder he said he was about to commit, appellant went to his girlfriend's place of employment. As she was walking to her car in the parking lot, he approached her, veered her away from the direction of her car, engaged her in a conversation, and finally shot her. He lifted her body into the passenger seat of his car and drove away. In his confession he stated that he thought the victim might still be alive, and he wanted to spend some time with her. He took her to a motel where they spent the night, and he made love to her. When the police found Santellan two days later the victim was deceased. The medical examiner testified at trial that the victim had probably died within minutes of the shooting.

Did the State prove that Santellan murdered his girlfriend during the commission of an attempted kidnapping? He argued that his actions did not amount to more than mere preparation for kidnapping prior to the victim's death. During the trial, the State agreed that a dead body could not be kidnapped, however, the acts amounting to more than mere preparation occurred when Santellan diverted the victim from her path to her automobile *before* her death.

The crime of kidnapping occurs under T.P.C. section 20.03 when a person intentionally or knowingly abducts another person. Abduct is defined in section 20.01(2):

> "Abduct" means to restrain a person with intent to prevent his liberty by:
> (A) secreting or holding him in a place where he is not likely to be found; or
> (B) using or threatening to use deadly force.

The Texas Court of Criminal Appeals started its analysis by concluding there was some evidence, despite the medical examiner's testimony, that the victim was alive for a little while after the shooting. The high court did not adopt the State's argument that the acts that went beyond preparation occurred when Santellan diverted his girlfriend in the parking lot. Texas case law has established that a kidnapper need not restrain a victim for any certain period of time. In addition, the law of attempt in Texas does not require that every act short of actual commission of the offense be accomplished. The Court of Criminal Appeals concluded that the appellant's act of loading the victim into the car and driving away with her was a sufficient act of restraint to amount to more than mere preparation.

Texas courts have not clearly announced in their opinions which one of the four tests is applicable in Texas for distinguishing mere preparation from criminal attempt: the physical proximity doctrine, the probable desistance doctrine, the equivocality approach, or the substantial steps/Model Penal Code standard. The courts have held that every act short of commission does not have to be performed for an attempted crime to have been committed, suggesting they reject the physical proximity test which requires the actor to have performed all but the last act to be guilty of an attempted offense. This chapter reviews some cases that indicate Texas judges have also rejected the probable desistance approach which asks whether an act ordinarily would lead to the commission of a crime but for timely interference. On the other hand, does the *Bledsoe* case support the probable desistance approach? It would be helpful if judges would always clearly define the legal doctrine on which they are relying. That is often not the case. Although never acknowledged directly, most of the cases reviewed in this chapter support the substantial steps standard.

> **Exercise:**
> Read the Texas kidnapping statutes in Chapter 20 of the Penal Code. Using the Court of Criminal Appeal's analysis in the *Santellan* case, could the appellant have been convicted of the completed crime of kidnapping? Since he was not charged with the completed crime in the indictment, he could not be convicted of it in his case according to the rules governing indictments. In retrospect, however, do you think the charge could have lead to a conviction? Why do you think the prosecutor did not charge him with the completed crime of kidnapping?

Specific Intent to Commit a Crime

Flanagan was convicted of attempted murder for shooting a gun while driving his car on the freeway at an off-duty police officer in his automobile, *Flanagan v. State*, 675 S.W.2d 734,741 (Tex. Crim. App. 1984). The officer was not injured. The court had to decide whether the shooting of a gun by a person in one automobile at another automobile, with both vehicles traveling at between 50 and 60 miles per hour, with the shot striking approximately the center of the front grill of the other vehicle, doing only slight damage, was sufficient evidence that the shooter had specific intent to kill the driver. Without specific intent to commit a murder, the appellant could not be convicted of attempted murder.

This case proved troublesome to the Texas Court of Criminal Appeals. They reviewed prior case law that held the intent to murder may be inferred from the use of a deadly weapon. Prior case law, however, also held that simply because a person shoots at another with a gun does not necessarily make it an assault with intent to murder. How the weapon was used, the type of shot fired, and the surrounding circumstances all have to be considered. The court decided that in this case there was insufficient evidence of intent to murder: the gun was fired from a significant distance at a speeding car, only slight damage was done to the car, and the driver was not injured. Although appellant's acts were reprehensible, the offense committed was not attempted murder.

The State asked the court to reconsider its finding. The State argued that the offense of murder does not require specific intent to kill, therefore, the court was incorrect in engrafting such intent onto the offense of attempted murder. All that is required is specific intent to cause serious bodily injury. Section 19.02(a) provides that a person commits murder if he:

(1) intentionally or knowingly causes the death of an individual;
(2) intends to cause serious bodily injury and commits an act clearly dangerous to human life that causes the death of an individual.

The court reconsidered its original finding but rejected the State's argument. It wrote about criminal attempt law:

> The element "with specific intent to commit an offense" has traditionally been interpreted to mean that the actor must have the intent to bring about the desired result, which in the case of attempted murder is the death of the individual.
> Thus, a specific intent to kill is a necessary element of attempted murder. The authorities in support of this interpretation are numerous and convincing.

Although the State's argument did not persuade the Court of Criminal Appeals, it decided to reconsider its first opinion for other reasons. The court concluded the opinion had failed to look at the totality of circumstances. The facts established at trial that the driver of the car under attack saw the appellant pick up a gun and aim it directly at him before pulling the trigger. The court's second opinion found there was sufficient evidence that Flanagan had specific intent to kill. Flanagan's conviction was upheld.

> **Exercise:**
> The *Flanagan* case is a good example of how reasonable and intelligent minds can differ, even among judges serving on the same court. Take a look at the aggravated assault statute in Texas and see how attempted murder and aggravated assault could overlap if the court had accepted the State's position.

Another attempted murder case, this time capital murder, raised interesting legal issues in *Godsey v. State*, 719 S.W.2d 578 (Tex. Crim. App. 1986). Godsey was convicted of attempting to murder a police officer. The Court of Appeals in San Antonio reversed his conviction because it believed the jury should have been permitted to consider the lesser-included offenses of aggravated assault and reckless conduct. Police arrived at Godsey's apartment complex after receiving reports that he was firing a gun into the air and had taken several people hostage. Twenty or so officers surrounded the area around his apartment. Godsey walked onto his apartment balcony with a pistol in his waistband. Police yelled for him not to touch the gun. He pulled it out and held it up, pointing it at various officers as he spotted them surrounding the complex grounds. He leveled it at two officers. Three officers then fired at him and knocked him down. Godsey testified at his trial that he had recently been released from a mental hospital and had gotten so drunk he did not remember confronting the officers.

Did Godsey have specific intent to kill the police? The Court of Criminal Appeals decided he did. The deliberate manner in which he took the gun from his waistband, ignored the officers' instructions to drop it, waived it around, and pointed it at two specific officers was sufficient evidence of his intent to kill. It was not necessary that he shoot the gun. The court reasoned that under certain circumstances, pointing a gun could amount to more than mere preparation to commit the offense of attempted murder.

> **Exercises:**
> Read *Sorce v. State*, 736 S.W.2d 851 (Tex. App. - Houston [14th Dist.] 1987). Appellant was convicted of attempted theft of property valued over $20,000 or more. Sorce, along with two other men, was involved in the sale of an herbal cancer treatment. Undercover police contacted him for information about the treatment. Sorce made false representations about its effectiveness. The police agent taped the conversations in which a $25,000 fee for the treatment was discussed. Appellant argued he could not be found guilty of attempted theft because theft by deception cannot occur if the supposed victim knew the representations were untrue. Did the court conclude that Sorce had the specific intent to deceive?
>
> Michael Epps was convicted of attempted burglary in *Epps v. State*, 811 S.W.2d 237 (Tex. App. - Dallas 1991). The facts showed that he removed the window screen of Jay Dolfuss's patio window. When Dolfuss discovered Epps, he was standing with a brick in his hand about to throw it at the now screenless window. Epps ran and was later arrested close to the scene. Did Epps commit attempted burglary? Did the court conclude there was sufficient evidence of his intent to commit the crime of burglary? What about criminal mischief?

CONSPIRING TO COMMIT A CRIME

Section 15.02 of the T.P.C. defines conspiracy:

(a) A person commits criminal conspiracy if, with intent that a felony be committed:
(1) he agrees with one or more persons that they or one or more of them engage in conduct that would constitute the offense; and
(2) he or one or more of them performs an overt act in pursuance of the agreement.
(b) An agreement constituting a conspiracy may be inferred from acts of the parties.

In Texas, criminal conspiracies involve agreements to commit only felonies and the agreement must be accompanied by an overt act in pursuance of the agreement. The overt act need not itself be of a criminal nature.

Cases Interpreting the Law of Conspiracy

Williams v. State, 646 S.W.2d 221 (Tex. Crim. App. 1984) is an important case defining the law of conspiracy in Texas. The Dallas police asked Steve Jennings, William's alleged coconspirator, to cultivate a friendship with the appellant and report any suspicious activity to them. Williams asked Jennings if he wanted to make some money by setting up a kidnapping of the son of the appellant's former employer. The ransom money would be split between them. Jennings agreed and details of the kidnapping were discussed further. Two days before the crime was to occur, Jennings contacted the police. The police wired Jennings for sound, and he met with the appellant. Williams was arrested after several conversations he had with Jennings were recorded. At the trial, Jennings testified that he never intended to go along with the kidnapping but was only acting as an agent for the police.

The Texas Court of Criminal Appeals examined whether there really was an agreement between the appellant Williams and Jennings to commit a crime. An agreement involves a union between two or more minds in a thing to be done. In this case, the court concluded there was no meeting of the minds because there was no criminal intent in the minds of both individuals. The court rejected the State's argument that section 15.02 was meant to adopt an entirely unilateral approach with each person's culpability determined without regard to the culpability of the alleged coconspirators. The reason conspiring to commit a felony is defined by statute as a separate crime is to attack the special danger that criminal combinations pose to society. Without such a combination based on a mutual agreement, there is no conspiracy.

The unilateral approach the State was referring to in *Williams* involves section 15.02(c):

It is no defense to prosecution for criminal conspiracy that:
(1) one or more of the coconspirators is not criminally responsible for the object offense;
(2) one or more of the coconspirators has been acquitted, so long as two or more coconspirators have not been acquitted;
(3) one or more of the coconspirators has not been prosecuted or convicted, has been convicted of a different offense, or is immune from prosecution;
(4) the actor belongs to a class of persons that by definition of the object offense is legally incapable of committing the object offense in an individual capacity; or
(5) the object offense was actually committed.

The court was not convinced to waive what it thought was the most essential requirement of conspiracy, a mutual and actual agreement to commit a felony. The Texas position is contrary to most states where conspiracy can be a unilateral crime.

Special Evidence Issues

A common issue in many criminal conspiracy, solicitation, and engaging in organized crime cases is raised when one of the coconspirators testifies against his or her "colleagues" in crime. Article 38.14 of the Texas Code of Criminal Procedure states:

A conviction cannot be had upon the testimony of an accomplice unless corroborated by other evidence tending to connect the defendant with the offense committed; and the corroboration is not sufficient if it merely shows the commission of the offense.

Texas courts have interpreted article 38.14 to mean that the testimony of an accomplice witness is sufficiently corroborated if, after eliminating that testimony from consideration, there is evidence that <u>tends to connect</u> the defendant with the crime. The corroborating evidence, however, does not need to link the defendant directly to the crime or be sufficient itself to establish guilt.

In *Butler v. State*, 758 S.W.2d 856 (Tex. App. - Houston [14th Dist.] 1988), the issue before the appeals court was the testimony of Dale Cureton against his coconspirator Jimmie Butler. While driving his car, Cureton was stopped by police who found guns, ammunition, gloves and masks in his vehicle. He and his companion told police they had been hired by Butler to kill his ex-wife's husband, and the equipment in the car was for that purpose. Cureton agreed to be wired and cooperated with the police. On tape he discussed the murder plans with Butler. Cureton testified at the trial when the taped conversations were introduced. The appellant argued on appeal that Cureton's testimony had not been sufficiently corroborated under article 38.14. The court disagreed and found that Cureton's testimony was amply corroborated by the discovery of the guns and equipment, the testimony of four other persons to whom he had mentioned his plans, and his own comments on tape.

In contrast, in *Morrison v. State*, 631 S.W.2d 242 (Tex. App. - Ft. Worth 1982), the accomplice witness testified at Morrison's trial that he had agreed to murder Ronald Adams for Morrison. Adams was to be killed because he was scheduled to testify against the appellant in a federal criminal trial. The police found out about the plot and asked the accomplice to wear a wire. He agreed and made additional murder plans with the appellant. At the trial, the accomplice identified Morrison's voice on the tape; however, no one else was able to corroborate the accomplice's testimony. Excluding the accomplice's testimony from consideration under article 38.14, there was no identification of the voices other than the accomplice's voice. The tape recording failed to connect the Morrison to the crime. The court ruled there was insufficient corroboration of the accomplice's testimony.

Section 71.02 Engaging in Organized Criminal Activity

Section 71.02, Engaging in Organized Criminal Activity, is an important companion statute to criminal conspiracy under section 15.02. In many ways it is far more comprehensive and sweeping than section 15.02.

> (a) A person commits an offense if, with intent to establish, maintain, or participate in a combination or in the profits of a combination or as a member of a criminal street gang, he commits or conspires to commit one or more of the following:
> (1) murder, capital murder, arson, aggravated robbery, robbery, burglary, theft, aggravated kidnapping, kidnapping, aggravated assault, aggravated sexual assault, sexual assault, forgery, deadly conduct, assault punishable as a Class A misdemeanor, burglary of a motor vehicle, or unauthorized use of a motor vehicle;
> (2) any gambling offenses punishable as a Class A misdemeanor;
> (3) promotion of prostitution, aggravated promotion of prostitution, or compelling prostitution;
> (4) unlawful manufacture, transportation, repair, or sale of firearms or prohibited weapons;
> (5) unlawful manufacture, delivery, dispensation, or distribution of a controlled substance or dangerous drug, or unlawful possession of a controlled substance or dangerous drug through forgery, fraud, misrepresentation, or deception;
> (6) any unlawful wholesale promotion or possession of any obscene material or obscene device with the intent to wholesale promote the same;
> (7) any offense under Subchapter B, Chapter 43, depicting or involving conduct by or directed toward a child younger than 18 years of age;
> (8) any felony offense under Chapter 32, Penal Code;
> (9) any offense under Chapter 36, Penal Code;
> (10) any offense under Chapter 34, Penal Code; or
> (11) any offense under Section 37.11(a), Penal Code.

Section 71.01 provides key definitions:

(a) "Combination" means three or more persons who collaborate in carrying on criminal activities, although:
(1) participants may not know each other's identity;
(2) membership in the combination may change from time to time; and
(3) participants may stand in a wholesaler-retailer or other arm's length relationship in illicit distribution operations.
(4) "Conspire to commit" means that a person agrees with one or more persons that they or one or more of them engage in conduct that would constitute the offense and that person and one or more of them perform an overt act in pursuance of the agreement. An agreement constituting conspiring to commit may be inferred from the acts of the parties.
(a) "Profits" means property constituting or derived from any proceeds obtained, directly or indirectly, from an offense listed in Section 71.02.
(b) "Criminal street gang" means three or more persons having a common identifying sign or symbol or an identifiable leadership who continuously or regularly associate in the commission of criminal activities.

Section 71.03 states that it is no defense to prosecution under section 71.02 that:

(1) one or more members of the combination are not criminally responsible for the object offense;
(2) one or more members of the combination have been acquitted, have not been prosecuted or convicted, have been convicted of a different offense, or are immune from prosecution;
(3) a person has been charged with, acquitted, or convicted of any offense listed in Subsection (a) of Section 71.02; or
(4) once the initial combination of three or more persons is formed there is a change in the number or identity of persons in the combination as long as two or more persons remain in the combination and are involved in a continuing course of conduct constituting an offense under this chapter.

The legislature carefully worded the statute to withstand challenges to its constitutionality, in particular whether it is void-for-vagueness or overbroad. The legislature has amended it several times to clarify certain terms and concepts and to strengthen its provisions. The original statute required a combination of five persons. That number has been reduced to three.

Texas' courts have also been instrumental in clarifying the statute's various provisions. The statute's constitutionality was upheld in *Lucario v. State*, 677 S.W.2d 693, 700 (Tex. App. - Houston [1 Dist.] 1984). Lucario was convicted of engaging in organized criminal activity as a result of his participation in an aggravated robbery ring. He complained that the mens rea element of section 71.02 fails to give sufficient notice of what conduct is criminal and fails to require that a person be aware that his activities are aiding an illegal combination. This allows people to be prosecuted who do not realize they are involved in illegal conduct. The court rejected his arguments and wrote:

The provisions concerning "collaboration in carrying on" would only apply if the requisite intent under the statute was established and would not include the lawful activity of a fiduciary or employee of a combination where the requisite intent is absent. Furthermore, the definition of a combination requires that the group of persons involved "collaborate" in carrying on a criminal activity. The scienter element of the offense requires that a person intend to establish, maintain, or participate in a group which collaborates in carrying on a criminal activity. ... The scienter element of the statute requires that the actor know of the criminal activity of the group.

The actus reus of engaging in organized crime is collaborating to carry on criminal activity. The Court of Criminal Appeals decided a recent case that refined the meaning of the actus reus requirement. In *Nguyen v. State*, 1 S.W.3d 694 (Tex. Crim. App. 1999) a tragic set of circumstances led to Nguyen being convicted of murder and engaging in organized criminal activity under section 71.02 of the Penal Code. Nguyen and a group of friends attended a party sponsored by the Asian Cultural Committee on the University of Texas campus. After the party they went to an Austin restaurant where a group four young men, including Jose de la Morena, were eating after attending a gathering of the UT Latin American Student Association. A woman from Nguyen's group walked past Morena's table when Morena allegedly asked her to show her nipples. She reported the remark to her friends. Before departing the restaurant, Nguyen and several of his group confronted Morena and demanded he step outside to fight. The police arrived and asked Nguyen and his friends to leave and Morena and his friends to leave as soon as their meal was finished. Nguyen left and with three other males and retrieved a semi-automatic rifle from his apartment. They returned to the restaurant to scare Morena. As Morena and his friends were leaving, Nguyen fired his rifle, shot and killed Morena and injured another man. Nguyen argued that the State inappropriately charged him under section 71.02 because he and his friends only collaborated to commit a single crime. He maintained that the language "collaborating in carrying on criminal activities" was meant to address activities that continue over time and involve more than a single act. The Court of Criminal Appeals agreed with Nguyen and his conviction under section 71.02 was overturned. The court was careful to note that a conviction under section 71.02 can rest on only one criminal offense as long as there is proof that there was an intent to carry on additional criminal activities. A conviction can also result if none of the enumerated offenses were committed as long as offender participated in committing an overt act.

In the case *Barber v. State*, 764 S.W.2d 232 (Tex. Crim. App. 1988), the Texas Court of Criminal Appeals explained the difference between sections 15.02 and 71.02. Section 71.01(b) defines "conspiring to commit" to mean that a person agrees with other persons that they or one of them will commit a crime and *that person and one or more of the others* must commit an overt act that furthers the agreement. Under section 15.02, a person can be guilty of criminal conspiracy by doing nothing more than agreeing to participate in a crime as long as someone involved in the conspiracy commits an overt act. To be guilty under section 71.02, however, the actor must not only agree to participate, he must perform an overt act. Another important difference is that one person alone cannot commit conspiracy. Under the organized crime statute, once at least three persons form a group to engage in crime, one of the three could be found guilty of forming a combination and two acquitted because they did not commit an overt act. Unlike criminal conspiracy law, one person alone can be guilty of engaging in organized criminal activity.

Section 71.02 has been used extensively in prosecuting drug-related offenses involving organized distribution networks. It has also been used in connection with loosely knit networks of sellers and wholesalers. In *Shears v. State*, 895 S.W.2d 456 (Tex. App.- Tyler 1995), the appellant was convicted of engaging in organized criminal activity by conspiring to commit the offense of unlawful delivery of a controlled substance. Police suspected Shears and others of selling crack cocaine from an apartment. They began a covert operation, videotaped the apartment complex, noting the cars coming and going, dates, and times. Finally, three officers went under cover and purchased cocaine from of the various sellers operating out of the same apartment, including Shears. Appellant argued there was insufficient evidence to show that he and the others agreed to work within a combination to sell drugs. The activities at the apartment were too loosely knit to comprise a combination. In fact, the dealers were competing against each other for profits.

The court was not persuaded. The taped video showed an extensive and busy drug distribution operation at the apartment. Shear actively participated in that operation, approaching cars, make exchanges, and going back and forth from the apartment delivering the drugs. Informants testified at trial that Shears sold drugs to make his living. Based on circumstantial evidence, the court ruled there were sufficient facts to establish a combination under the law.

A similar set of circumstances occurred in *Caddell v. State*, 902 S.W.2d 554 (Tex. App. - Tyler 1995). Caddell was convicted of engaging in organized activity to distribute drugs. He sold drugs in an open field in Tyler, Texas called the "Graveyard." Police videotapes documented large numbers of drug transactions occurring there on a daily basis. Caddell sold drugs to several undercover police officers. He argued there was no criminal combination. The court pointed to the existence of a loosely organized drug market that evidenced a tacit agreement among the sellers. The sales took place in a common area, at a common time, using a common method, from the practice of selling for others and giving warnings when the police entered the area. There was a common "burn barrel," where contraband would be thrown and destroyed in the event of a raid. The court concluded that the jury could rationally decide that these were not discreet, unrelated drug transactions, but constituted a criminal collaboration with a common purpose.

On a non-drug related note, a case that raised some First Amendment issues, *Brosky v. State*, 915 S.W.2d 120 (Tex. App. - Ft. Worth 1996) concerned a young man found guilty of engaging in organized criminal activity to commit murder. He and two friends involved in the skinhead movement decided to kill an African-American. They drove around the streets of Arlington in an automobile, looking for a victim. They shot and killed a black man who they did not know, nor had they met. Brosky complained on appeal that his political beliefs should not have been introduced into evidence and that he had been convicted of participating in a combination that had unpopular opinions about race issues. In upholding Brosky's conviction, the court emphasized that he participated in a combination that planned a murder and performed overt acts to further the plan by riding in the car, encouraging the shooting, and destroying evidence after the crime was committed.

> **Exercise:**
> See the companion cases to *Caddell v. State*: *Rainey v. State*, 877 S.W.2d 48 (Tex. App. - Tyler 1994) and *Mayfield v. State*, 906 S.W.2d 46 (Tex. App. - Tyler 1995). All three cases involve activities at the "Graveyard." The defendants, however, each played a slightly different role in the drug distribution business.
>
> Compare the punishment for conspiracy to commit robbery (sections 15.02 and 29.01 of the T.P.C.), engaging in organized criminal activity to commit robbery (sections 71.02 and 29.01), and the actual crime of committing robbery (section 29.01). Notice how severe the sanction is for engaging in organized criminal activity. Why do you think the legislature made the punishment so severe?

CRIMINAL SOLICITATION

Section 15.03 of the T.P.C. addresses criminal solicitation and makes it a crime to request, demand or attempt to induce another person to engage in conduct that would constitute a felony. Unlike conspiracy and attempt law, there is no requirement that an overt act be committed. The criminal mens rea requires the intent to commit a capital felony or a felony of the first degree. The statute provides that a person cannot be convicted of solicitation on the uncorroborated testimony of the person solicited. There must be evidence strongly corroborative of the solicitation and the solicitor's intent that the person he solicited actually commit the crime. By setting high standards of proof, the State hopes to weed out cases involving set-ups and to tap only genuine criminal activity, not just wishful, half-hearted thinking. The offense of solicitation is complete once a request or inducement is <u>unilaterally</u> presented. Unlike conspiracy crimes, there is no requirement of a meeting of the minds.

Section 15.031 makes it a separate offense to solicit a minor to commit a crime listed in Section 3g(a)(1) of Article 42.12 of the Texas Code of Criminal Procedure. For the purposes of section 15.031, a minor is under 17 years old. "Section 3(g)" offenses include: capital murder, murder, indecency with a child, aggravated kidnapping, aggravated sexual assault, and aggravated robbery. As a group, these offenses have been labeled "3(g) offenses" and appear as a group throughout the Code of Criminal Procedure. Offenders convicted of a crime included in this group earn reduced good time in prison and have limited opportunities available for receiving probated sentences. The 76th Texas legislature further amended section 15.031 to make it a crime to solicit a minor to commit a sexual performance with another child. The statute's goal is to provide severe and certain punishment for adults who use minors to commit crimes on their behalf or for their enjoyment.

A very recent addition to the arsenal of solicitation crimes in Texas is section 71.022. The new law makes it a crime to knowingly cause, enable, encourage, recruit, or solicit a person to become a member of a criminal street gang if a condition of initiation, admission or membership requires that person to commit any crime that is a Class A misdemeanor or felony. The term "criminal street gang" is defined as three or more persons that have a common identifying sign, symbol, or leadership and who continuously engage in committing crime.

Section 71.022 is located in the chapter of the penal code reserved for organized crime and addresses many of the same concerns that caused the legislature to adopt the organized crime statute.

FINAL COMMENTS ON INCHOATE CRIMES

Section 15.04 of the T.P.C. allows an accused to plead a renunciation defense to prosecution for any of the crimes charged under section 15.01. The accused must show that he or she voluntarily and completely renounced their criminal objective, thereby avoiding the commission of the crime or, if that was not possible, took affirmative action to prevent its commission. Renunciation is not voluntary if it was motivated by circumstances that were not present or apparent at the beginning of the criminal project that would have increased the probability of detection or apprehension or would make it more difficult to accomplish the objective. Renunciation also does not cover those instances when the perpetrator decides to postpone the crime until another time or with another victim. As an affirmative defense, the Penal Code section 2.04 requires that the defendant prove renunciation by a preponderance of the evidence.

MULTIPLE CHOICE QUESTIONS

1. Dick decided to rob the Megabucks Bank across town and approached his two friends, Hank and Oscar, for their participation. They agreed and the planning process began. Hank purchased the ski masks and the tape and rope. Oscar had friends who sold him the weapons. Unfortunately, before Dick could reconnoiter the bank (his assignment) and scope out the right time of day and escape route, the police found out about their plans. Oscar told his wife who went to the police. The three had never been involved together in criminal activity. This was their first group effort. The D.A. has to decide what to charge them with. He starts with Dick, the acknowledged leader and inspiration for the group.

    a. Dick can be charged with engaging in organized criminal activity under section 71.02.
    b. Dick cannot be charged with a crime under section 71.02 and the D.A. should consider section 15.02.
    c. Dick can be charged under section 15.02 and 71.02.
    d. Dick is not guilty of a crime since none was attempted.

2. After discovering that his wife had reported him to the authorities for his role in the Megabucks Bank scheme, Oscar decided to bump off his wife. Before going to prison, he contacted a friend and together they planned. Oscar wrote up a map with detailed directions and instructions about how the crime should be committed. Unfortunately, the friend turned out to be an undercover police officer. Can the D.A. charge Oscar with conspiracy?

    a. Yes, he reached an agreement with the officer.
    b. Yes, he reached an agreement and performed an overt act in furtherance of it.
    c. No, he can not conspire with a police officer.
    d. No, because the officer also has to commit an overt act.

3. Hank also decided to bump off Oscar's wife, who he never particularly liked. He contacted a "real" friend and requested he commit the job. The friend refused because Hank could only pay $1000.00. The friend thought a murder was worth at least $5000. Hank figured he wouldn't find a decent murderer for $1000, so he dropped the idea. Hank's friend was a blabbermouth and told about Hank's offer. Word filtered back to the police who arrested Hank for criminal solicitation. There was no other evidence but the friend's testimony. Can he be charged with the crime?

   a. Yes, it does not matter that the person he solicited refused.
   b. No, no overt acts were committed.
   c. No, there is no evidence to corroborate the friend's testimony.
   d. Yes, because the friend obviously has no ax to grind against Hank, otherwise he would have gone directly to the police.

4. Dick decided to take matters into his own hands and wipe out Oscar's wife once and for all. He decided to do the job himself, without consultation or assistance. He watched Oscar's house and noted the wife's coming and goings. He procured a weapon. He followed her around town and got to know her schedule. Finally, he was ready. He was ready to jump her one morning as she walked to her car in the parking lot of the apartment complex. It was 5 a.m. and no one was watching, or so he thought. Just as he was about to dash at her from the bushes where he was hiding, he noticed she had a large German shepherd dog by her side. The dog looked very ferocious, and Dick stopped in his tracks. He was dressed in army fatigues and had his gun pulled. A neighbor watched the entire scene from her balcony and called the police who got there before Dick could make a getaway. Oscar's wife never saw Dick coming.

   a. Dick is guilty of attempted murder.
   b. Dick is just short of being guilty of attempted murder because he is still in the mere preparation stage.
   c. Dick abandoned the attack. He's not guilty of anything, just lucky.
   d. Dick is guilty of harassing Oscar's wife.

5. A person cannot be convicted of criminal attempt if the crime was actually committed.

   a. True
   b. False

6. If Dick and Oscar are acquitted of criminal conspiracy in the scenario above, Hank cannot be convicted of criminal conspiracy.

   a. True
   b. False

7. A person cannot be convicted of criminal solicitation if the felony was actually committed.

   a. True
   b. False

8. It is necessary that the participants to a combination engaging in organized crime know each other's identity.

    a. True
    b. False

9. In a case under section 71.02 of the T.P.C., a participant in the combination does not have to commit an overt act themselves in order to be found guilty under that statute.

    a. True
    b. False

10. In a case under section 71.02, at least how many people must commit overt acts for a participant to be found guilty?

    a. at least 4
    b. at least 1 - the participant who has been charged
    c. at least 2 - one of whom must be the participant being charged
    d. at least 1- any one, not necessarily the participant charged

CHAPTER SEVEN

DEFENSES TO CRIMINAL LIABILITY: JUSTIFICATIONS

INTRODUCTION

Defenses to criminal charges raise some of the most controversial questions of law and often implicate broader public policy concerns. Chapter Seven examines defenses to criminal charges in the form of justifications, concentrating on two major justification defenses:

1) self-defense, including all the variations of defense of third parties and defenses of property, and
2) the necessity or choice of evils defense.

In the case of self-defense, how do we vigorously protect a citizen's right to self-defense without encouraging a spirit of vigilante justice? To what extent do we want citizens to defend their property? Is it always better to kill the intruder? Is it safe for property owners to use force to defend their property? Texas has a reputation for liberally applying the right to defend oneself and one's property. Is that reputation deserved?

In certain fact situations, the necessity of evils defense is related to a defense of coercion discussed in Chapter Eight. This chapter will look at the narrow interpretation the courts have placed on the necessity defense. A necessity defense can also involve a court in a tough decision that has ramifications beyond the facts of an individual case.

SELF-DEFENSE

Because self-defense raises many issues, this section of Chapter Seven is divided into several distinct subject matter areas. Self-defense statutes are lengthy and convoluted, so they have been rearranged and slightly re-worded from the Penal Code format to make for easier reading. Many cases present more than one issue for a court to consider that are usually hard to separate and often overlap. Using deadly force to defend oneself can also involve the right to defend property or a third person.

Non-Deadly Force

Section 9.31 of the T.P.C. provides that a defendant is justified in using force to protect himself against another person when and to the degree he <u>reasonably believes</u> it is <u>immediately necessary</u> to protect himself from another person's use or attempted use of <u>unlawful</u> force.

Deadly Force

A defendant is justified in deadly force in self-defense if he is justified in using force under section 9.31 and:

(1) If a reasonable person in the defendant's situation would not have retreated; and
(2) When and to the degree he reasonably believes the deadly force is immediately necessary:
- to protect himself against the other person's use or attempted use of unlawful deadly force; or
- to prevent the other person's imminent commission of aggravated kidnapping, murder, sexual assault, aggravated sexual assault, robbery, or aggravated robbery.
- Except theses limitations do not apply when a defendant uses force against a person who at the time is committing an offense of unlawful entry in the defendant's habitation.

Defense of a Third Person

Non-deadly and deadly force can be used by a defendant to protect a third person under section 9.33 if the defendant would have been justified in using force under sections 9.31 or 9.32 to protect himself against the force being used against the third person, and he believes that his intervention is immediately necessary to protect the third person.

Burden of Proof

Section 2.03 of the T.P.C. gives the State the burden of proof on the self-defense issue. Once the defendant argues self-defense, defense of a third person or defense of property, the State's job is to disprove that claim beyond a reasonable doubt. This means the court must charge the jury that if the State has not shown beyond a reasonable doubt that the defendant was not acting in self-defense, they should decide for acquittal.

If a defendant raises any proof during trial that supports his self-defense claim, he is entitled to a jury instruction on the issue. A jury instruction explains to the jury what the law is in Texas about a specific matter and instructs the members of the jury to apply the law to the particular facts of the case they are considering. It does not matter whether the evidence supporting the claim is strong or weak. The credibility of the evidence or whether it conflicted with other evidence does not matter. Those are issues for a jury to weigh. The defendant does not even have to testify during the trial in order for there to be enough evidence that he or she acted in self-defense.

A Reasonable Belief

Using deadly force is only justified if the defendant reasonably believed deadly force was immediately necessary to protect himself against the actual or attempted use of unlawful deadly force or to prevent the commission of certain violent crimes. Section 1.07(42) of the Texas Penal Code defines "reasonable belief" as a belief that would be held by an ordinary and prudent person in the same circumstances as the defendant.

The court ruled that a blow to the face with an open or closed hand does not give rise to the use of deadly force in *Ogas v. State*, 655 S.W.2d 322 (Tex. App. - Amarillo 1983). In that case, a pregnant woman shot a man after he slapped her. The appeals court decided that non-deadly force might have been justified, but not deadly force. A slap to the face that did not threaten the fetus failed to support the claim that the woman reasonably feared death or serious bodily injury. Without other threats, a blow to the head struck by a hand did not convince the court that the defendant reasonably believed deadly force was necessary in *Molitor v. State*, 827 S.W.2d 512 (Tex. App. - Austin 1992).

Texas case law suggests that courts should use an objective standard to determine whether a person was reasonable in using deadly force in self-defense. Under an objective standard, the defendant is judged by what a reasonable person in the same or similar circumstances would have believed was necessary. In contrast is the subjective standard which focuses on what the defendant honestly believed at the time was necessary for protection.

In recent years, the Texas Court of Criminal Appeals has been somewhat inconsistent in explaining the reasonableness standard. Several cases decided in the 1970s set forth a subjective standard. They held that reasonableness should be judged from the accused person's standpoint at the instant he responds to an attack. In *Valentine v. State*, 587 S.W.2d 399 (Tex Crim. App. 1979), however, the court moved to an objective standard to affirm a wife's manslaughter conviction against a claim of self-defense. In that case, Valentine shot and killed her husband through the locked door of their trailer home. He had been pounding on the door, shouting obscenities, and threatening to kill her and had a history of violence toward her. The court ruled that the subjective standard was not applicable. *Valentine*, however, was followed by several cases that seemed to return to the subjective approach.

It now appears that the Court of Criminal Appeals has moved to a blend of the two standards. In *Werner v. State,* 711 S.W.2d 639 (Tex Crim. App. 1986), the court held that determining whether deadly force was justifiable requires evaluating 1) whether the defendant acted on appearances from his own standpoint in deciding whether force was immediately necessary, and 2) whether an ordinary prudent person in the defendant's situation would have retreated. In *Werner*, the defendant witnessed the victim run into a parked car. When the victim did not stop, Werner pursued him. He could not see the victim's hands and could not tell if he was carrying a weapon. Werner said he feared for his life and shot the victim. Other recent self-defense cases also evaluate reasonableness by viewing the circumstances from the defendant's standpoint at the time and using a prudent/reasonable person approach.

Texas case law is clear that a person has the right to defend herself against apparent danger to the same extent as actual danger. It does not matter that the defendant's evaluation of the danger was incorrect, as long as the perception of danger was reasonable.

Evidence of the victim's general reputation for being violent and the victim's prior acts of violence is admissible. This type of evidence helps establish that the defendant was reasonable in claiming he was in fear. *Halliburton v. State*, 528 S.W.2d 216 (Tex Crim. App. 1975) provides an example of how other violent offenses can be used to establish who was the aggressor. Halliburton shot and killed her common law husband, claiming he had threatened to kill her. There were no witnesses. Evidence was introduced at trial that five weeks after she shot her husband, Halliburton shot and injured a man who owed her money and was unable to pay. The court ruled that the second shooting was admissible to help establish whether she or her husband had been the aggressor in the first shooting.

> **Exercises:**
> Read *Ex Parte Dinkert*, 821 S.W.2d 953 (Tex Crim. App. 1991). Dinkert shot and killed his son's friend who he thought was breaking into his house. Read *Kolliner v. State*, 516 S.W.2d 671 (Tex Crim. App. 1974). Kolliner killed a police officer who he mistakenly thought was going to shoot him. He testified that he did not realize the victim was an officer. Both cases address the reasonableness of the defendants' beliefs.
>
> Find other Texas cases interpreting the reasonableness standard for the use of deadly force in self-defense. You can see why actually seeing witnesses testify in order to examine their demeanor, voice inflection and body language is essential. That's why appellate courts defer to jury decisions.

Limitations on Self-Defense

Section 9.31 places limits on self-defense that apply to both non-deadly and deadly uses of force:

(1) In response to verbal provocation alone;
(2) To resist an arrest or search that the defendant knows is being made by a peace officer, or someone acting in the officer's presence and at his direction, even if the arrest and/or search is unlawful, except if prior to the defendant's resistance, the peace officer or his representative uses or attempts to use force greater than that which is necessary to make the arrest or conduct the search, and the defendant reasonably believes force is necessary to protect himself;
(3) If the defendant consented to the exact force used or attempted by the other person;
(4) If the other person's actual or attempted use of unlawful force was in response to provocation by the defendant, unless:
> the defendant abandons the encounter or, believing he cannot safely abandon it clearly communicates his intention to do so; and
> the other person continues to actually use or attempt to use unlawful force against the defendant;
(5) If the defendant sought an explanation from or a discussion with the other person concerning the defendant's differences with the other person while the defendant was:
> carrying a weapon in violation of Section 46.02 of the T.P.C.: or
> possessing or transporting a weapon in violation of Section 46.05 of the T.P.C.

To Resist Arrest

An important limitation on self-defense involves searches and arrests conducted by law enforcement officers or their agents. There is no right to self-defense during an arrest or search even if the officer is acting unlawfully. The only exception is if the officer is using excessive force before the defendant offers any resistance. Of course, as in all self-defense situations, the defendant must have reasonably believed that self-defense was immediately necessary. This limitation also requires the defendant know that the person attempting to arrest or search him is a peace officer or an agent of an officer.

Aguilar v. State, 914 S.W.2d 649 (Tex. App. - Texarkana 1996), raised the issue of self-defense against an officer's excessive use of force. Aguilar was arguing with his girlfriend. Officers saw him hanging from the front door of her car as she was driving out of a restaurant parking lot. They stopped the car to question the couple. The officers testified that Aguilar appeared intoxicated, became loud and belligerent, pulled away to avoid being handcuffed and struck one of the officers. They shot pepper spray in his face to subdue him. At his trial for resisting arrest, Aguilar's girlfriend testified that he was not belligerent and was thrown to the ground and sprayed for no reason. The trial court refused to instruct the jury on the right of self-defense against a police officer who uses excessive force. The Court of Appeals reversed Aguilar's conviction. Evidence was introduced at trial suggesting that the officers had used excessive force. The credibility of the evidence was for the jury to decide, and an instruction on self-defense was warranted.

In contrast to *Aguilar* is *Evans v. State*, 876 S.W.2d 459 (Tex. App. - Texarkana 1994). Evans was convicted of aggravated assault of a police officer. The trial court had also refused to instruct the jury on self-defense. Evans claimed that an officer stopped him for an expired inspection sticker as he pulled up to his residence. He refused to produce proof of insurance, arguing he was on private property and did not have to cooperate with the police. The officer wrote several tickets, which Evans refused to accept. When the officer attempted to arrest him, he walked toward his front door. The officer grabbed Evans' arm to try to pin it against his back. Evans broke free and struck the officer with his elbow. The two fell to the ground and broke into a fistfight. In this case, the appellate court did not reverse and order jury instructions on self-defense because the evidence did not raise self-defense as a real issue. The officer's attempt to pin Evans' arm behind his back was justified because Evans refused arrest. There was no evidence that the officer used or attempted to use excessive force.

In both cases, the appellants challenged the force used by police. In the *Aguilar* case, there was eyewitness testimony that the police were excessive. It was for the jury to decide the credibility of the girlfriend's testimony. In *Evans*, the evidence was the defendant's version of events versus the officer's version. Evans admitted trying to avoid arrest and refusing the tickets. The officer had a lawful right to use some force to arrest him. The facts were not strong enough for the court to reverse his conviction.

Provoking the Difficulty

Probably the most important limitation on self-defense is "provoking the difficulty." Section 9.31(b)(4) provides that self-defense is not available to a defendant who provoked the victim into using or attempting to use unlawful force. In Texas, a trial judge will charge the jury on provoking the difficulty if:

(1) self-defense is an issue in the case;
(2) there are facts in evidence that show the victim made the first attack against the defendant; and
(3) there are facts in evidence that show the defendant did some act or used some words intended to and calculated to bring on the difficulty in order to have a pretext for injuring the victim.

A defendant can provoke the difficulty through words alone. It is not necessary to show the defendant used force or a threat of force in order to conclude the defendant provoked the victim into a first attack. Before a judge can inform the jury about the provoking the difficulty limitation, however, there must be some evidence that the defendant intended to provoke. If he or she did not intend to provoke the victim into attacking, their right to defend themselves is not limited.

In *Matthews v. State*, 708 S.W.2d 835 (Tex Crim. App. 1986), a 29-year old man was convicted of murdering a 75-year old man. The victim was a realtor who was negotiating a land sale to Matthews. Matthews testified that he was arguing with the victim about the sale price when the victim pulled out a gun, pointed it at him, and ordered him to leave his office. Matthews lost his head and grabbed the gun away from the realtor. He then pulled out his knife and stabbed the realtor to death. Matthews argued he acted in self-defense, that he had never intended to provoke an altercation although his words may have angered the realtor into displaying a weapon. After examining all the evidence, the court found there was reason to believe that Matthews intended to provoke the victim into attacking him first. Matthews stole $500 from the victim after he killed him, and there was evidence he was having financial problems. There was also reason to doubt whether Matthews was serious about purchasing the land the victim showed him. The court concluded that the jury should be advised about the provoking the difficult limitation and permitted to evaluate the facts.

Sometimes it is difficult to know who provoked whom. If you believe Thomas in *Thomas V. State*, 750 S.W.2d 324, 325 (Tex. App. – Dallas 1988), every family member was armed with a gun and more than willing to waive them about. John Thomas was not getting along well with his wife Shirley and his mother-in-law. Shirley Thomas decided to leave John and was packing up her belongings with the help of her mother and her daughter from a previous marriage. John testified at his trial for involuntary manslaughter that his mother-in-law cursed him and told him they were taking as much as they could from the house. At one point his stepdaughter pulled a gun on him and said she had wanted to kill him for a long time and shot at him. He also testified that his mother-in-law had shot at him with a shotgun on a previous occasion. The court's opinion goes on:

> He [appellant] ran, got his gun from under the mattress of the bed and looked around to shoot at the stepdaughter, but she had left the room. He then stated he was going to put his gun back but saw his mother-in-law sitting in a chair in another part of the same room. He testified that he knew she always carried a gun. She cursed at him again and accused him of desiring to shoot the stepdaughter, and he then observed her reaching down to pick up a foil package. He said he knew that the package contained a gun so he fired a shot at Mrs. Johnson's hands, although he did not see a gun in her hand. At this point, his wife Shirley came to the middle of the room and exclaimed "you shot my mama and I'll kill you" and reached into her bra where he believed she had a gun. Appellant testified that he leaped toward her to get the gun from her and during the struggle she was shot and killed. Although he was "almost positive" she had a gun, he never saw one nor was one found.

Thomas argued self-defense and contested the judge's decision to issue a jury charge on provoking the difficulty. The appeals court decided there was enough evidence to issue a charge that limited Thomas's right of self-defense because there was reason to believe he had provoked the encounter with his wife by first shooting his mother-in-law. The jury could reach the conclusion that shooting his wife's mother was a pretext for attacking his wife.

> **Exercise:**
> In the *Thomas* case, can you see how confusing and convoluted some of these fact situations can get? With angry people yelling and cursing at each other, issues of provoking the difficulty can be hard to untangle. Judges may feel most comfortable issuing the provoking jury instruction and letting the jury decide.
>
> Find other cases where self-defense was raised by looking at Vernon's Annotated Statutes and reading the case annotations listed following the self-defense statute. Get the case citation and find the case in the South Western Reporters. Notice the many different fact situations presented by the cases. Compare cases and see if you can tell why in some cases self-defense is more plausible than in others.

The Common Law Right to Arm Oneself

If the trial judge limits a defendant's right to self-defense by giving the jury an instruction on provoking the difficulty, Texas case law requires that the jury should also be instructed about the right to arm oneself. Under Texas common law, a person has the right to carry arms to the scene of a difficulty. In other words, a person's right to self-defense is not limited by the fact that he or she carried a weapon when they sought an explanation or attempted to resolve a problem with another person. The jury is advised of the "right to arm and seek an explanation" only if:

(1) there are facts in evidence that the defendant was armed when he sought a resolution; and
(2) the judge has instructed the jury that they must evaluate whether the defendant provoked the victim into attacking him first.

An instruction on the right to arm oneself is intended to make certain that a jury not conclude the defendant provoked the difficulty because he was armed when he went to meet with the victim. The common law in Texas protects the right of citizens to carry arms when they reasonably anticipate the potential need to defend themselves. In 1994, the legislature added a new provision abolishing the common law right to arm oneself if the defendant was carrying a weapon in violation of section 46.02 of the Texas Penal Code or possessing or transporting a weapon in violation of section 46.05.

Duty to Retreat

One of the most drastic changes in the 1974 Texas Penal Code was the adoption of the duty to retreat in section 9.32(2) which requires that before deadly force can be used in self-defense, the defendant must retreat if a reasonable person in his or her situation would have retreated. Retreat was not necessary to the right of self-defense in the old penal code. In fact, the old statute specifically provided that there was no duty to retreat.

The duty to retreat is triggered by section 9.31 if a reasonable person in the defendant's situation would have retreated. The word "situation" means a combination of circumstances at a given moment. Whether the defendant had the ability and opportunity to retreat is considered a part of the circumstances. In 1995, the legislature added new language to the duty to retreat provision. The new language removes the duty to retreat when the victim was unlawfully entering a habitation at the time the defendant used deadly force in self-defense. The change reflects the legislature's concern that persons who use deadly force against house burglars not be subjected to a court inquiry as to whether, under the circumstances, they should have retreated from their homes. The new provision, however, does not eliminate the duty to retreat from one's own home under circumstances other than a burglary.

Family Violence

In 1991 the Texas Legislature enacted a new law to address domestic violence cases involving battered spouses who kill their spouse-abusers, amending section 19.06 of the Penal Code. Up until 1991, in murder and voluntary manslaughter cases in which the defendant raised self-defense, section 19.06 allowed evidence to be introduced concerning the previous relationship between the accused and the deceased along with all the relevant circumstances surrounding the killing. The new amendment expanded 19.06 to allow evidence to be introduced that the accused had been the victim of family violence at the hands of the deceased, as defined by section 71.01 of the Family Code. The amendment also allows relevant expert testimony to be introduced concerning the condition of the accused's mind at the time of the offense, including facts and circumstances relating to family violence that were the basis of the expert's opinion.

The 1991 legislation came on the heels of an important domestic violence case, *Fielding v. State*, 756 S.W.2d 309 (Tex Crim. App. 1988). The jury convicted Fielding of voluntary manslaughter for killing her husband. There were facts that showed Fielding had suffered severe physical and sexual sadomasochistic abuse at the hands of her gynecologist husband. On several occasions, he threatened to kill her if she disclosed his sexual practices and abuse. On the day of the killing, Fielding told her husband she had contacted a divorce attorney. He became furious and abusive. He pulled her inside when she tried to leave their home. He got a pistol and slammed it on the table. She grabbed the gun and started to walk away from him. When he came toward her, she killed him. The State argued that Fielding was in a jealous rage because she had learned her husband was having an affair.

The defense wanted to introduce testimony from a psychologist as to why Fielding remained in a physically and sexually abusive relationship. The trial court refused. The appeals court reversed Fielding's conviction and ruled that it was error to refuse evidence that addressed the reasons for Fielding's fear and how it impacted her behavior. The issue of her fear was important because it addressed the statute's requirement that a person reasonably believe it was immediately necessary to defend themselves. The Criminal Court of Appeals decision in the *Fielder* case was an important impetus to expanding the law of self-defense in Texas.

Exercise:
Read section 71.01 of the Texas Family Code for the definition of family violence. Skim the entire chapter 71 to understand more about how civil courts use protective orders to help protect family members against family violence. Notice there are criminal penalties for violating a protective order that can lead to fines, jail, or prison confinement. Although civil courts issue protective orders, they involve criminal justice issues and their enforcement relies on law enforcement agencies.

Self-Defense in the Punishment Phase

Criminal trials in Texas are bifurcated. The first part of a trial determines the guilt or innocence of the accused. If the accused is found guilty, the second part of the trial determines punishment. During the penalty phase, both the defendant and the State can offer evidence relevant to matters of sentencing, including evidence about the defendant's prior criminal history, general reputation in the community, character, and the circumstances surrounding the offense. If a trial judge decides during the guilt or innocence phase that a defendant's evidence on self-defense is not sufficient for a charge to the jury, evidence about self-defense can be brought up during the punishment phase to mitigate the severity of punishment.

> **Exercise:**
> Review Chapter 37 of the Texas Code of Criminal Procedure concerning verdicts in criminal trials. Notice that convicted criminal defendants in Texas can elect to have their punishment decided by a judge or a jury. What factors do you think would enter into that decision? Under what circumstances would a defendant prefer to have a judge decide his or her fate?

Defense of Third Persons

Much of the law defining the right to self-defense is applicable to defending a third person. There must be an actual or apparent attack on the other person, and the defendant must reasonably believe his intervention is immediately necessary. At issue, then, are the circumstances of the third person and the defendant's state of mind. It is not necessary that the defendant and the third person be related for the defense to be successful. There is no duty to retreat before using deadly force to defend another person. To require otherwise would mean leaving the other person to the assailant's attack.

DEFENSE OF PROPERTY

Non-Deadly Force

Section 9.41 of the T.P.C. provides that a person who is lawfully in possession of real or tangible personal property is justified in using non-deadly force to prevent or terminate another person's trespass upon or unlawful interference with the property when and to the degree he reasonably believes the force is immediately necessary. A person who has been unlawfully dispossessed of property may reenter the real property or recover the personal property if he uses the force immediately or in fresh pursuit after the dispossession and:

(1) The defendant reasonably believes the other person had no claim of right when he dispossessed the defendant; or
(2) the other person accomplished the dispossession by using force, threat of force, or fraud against the defendant.

Deadly Force

To be justified in using deadly force to protect your real or personal property, you must first be justified in using non-deadly force under section 9.41; and

(1) When and to the degree the defendant reasonably believes the deadly force is immediately necessary:
to prevent the other person's imminent commission of arson, burglary, robbery, aggravated robbery, theft during the nighttime, or criminal mischief during the nighttime; or
to prevent the other person from fleeing immediately after committing one of those crimes and escaping with the property; and
(2) The defendant reasonably believes that:
the land or property cannot be protected or recovered by any other means; or
the use of force other than deadly force to protect or recover the property would expose the defendant or another to a substantial risk of death or serious bodily injury.

In *Hernandez v. State*, 914 S.W.2d 218 (Tex. App.- El Paso 1996), Danny Hernandez's home was the target of a drive-by shooting. Hernandez was a couple blocks away when it occurred, but he heard the shots and saw a white Monte Carlo speed away. Members of his family were in the home at the time of the shooting but no one was injured. Hernandez and six friends jumped into a car and went looking for the Monte Carlo. A high-speed chase ensued once they found it, and shots were exchanged. One of the occupants of the Monte Carlo died as a result of a gunshot wound to the head. Hernandez argued that he should have received a jury instruction on the issue of defense of property because his home had been shot at and he testified he was concerned that the perpetrators might return to harm his family. The appeals court, however, found there was no evidence that the Monte Carlo perpetrators were going to engage in additional criminal mischief, much less that it was imminent. Besides the drive-by shooting occurred prior to Hernandez's use of deadly force.

> **Exercise:**
> In an article appearing on March 8, 1994, the Houston Chronicle reported a tragic story about a case of defense of property. A 13-year old boy was fatally shot by Gerald Zeigler, a frightened homeowner. Zeigler decided to plead guilty to murder and received ten years deferred adjudication with the further requirement that he attend two meetings with victims' groups. The story reported:
>
> The case against Zeigler, 45, began in the early morning hours of October 1990, when the disabled Air Force veteran said he heard someone in his truck around 3:30 a.m. and went out to investigate. He confronted Silby, who then threw a brick at Zeigler's head and fled on his 10-speed bicycle. Silby was shot in the back as he pedaled away.
>
> Prosecutor Connie Spence said evidence about what Silby was actually doing around Zeigler's truck is conflicting. They surmise that Silby ventured out early that morning to sneak out on a camping trip with a friend, she said. He passed by Zeigler's house on the way for a soft drink, then returned, stopping by Zeigler's truck for some unknown reason. The lit dome light inside suggested Silby may have tampered with the vehicle, she said. "But I don't know why he was there."
>
> Zeigler's attorney, Randy McDonald, said his client was already in a heightened state of fear when Silby rode up his drive. His Spring neighborhood was on edge because of repeated reports of prowlers and a Peeping Tom. Zeigler had climbed onto his roof on several nights to keep watch.
>
> Pointing out that the brick thrown by Silby could have been deadly, McDonald said Zeigler was protecting both his property and himself when he fired at the teen. Although Zeigler felt justified in his actions, McDonald said his client has been distraught ever since. "He has been unable to talk about it without breaking up," McDonald said. His client never realized he was shooting at a young boy, and even tried to resuscitate the boy.
>
> Zeigler entered the guilty plea to help "put it behind him, for his family and the boy's," McDonald said.

Defending a Third Person's Property

Section 9.43 of the T.P.C. allows a defendant to use non-deadly or deadly force to protect the real or personal property of a third person if, under the circumstances as he believes them to be, he would be justified in using force to protect his own property; and he reasonably believes that the third person requested his protection of the property, he has a legal duty to protect the property, or the third person is the defendant's spouse, parent, or child, resides with him or is under his care.

> **Exercises:**
> Read *Sledge v. State*, 507 S.W.2d 726 (Tex Crim. App. 1974); *Warren v. State*, 764 S.W.2d 906 (Tex. App. - Corpus Christi 1989); *Molitor v. State*, 827 S.W.2d 512 (Tex. App. - Austin 1992); *Banks v. State*, 624 S.W.2d 762 (Tex. App. - Houston [14th Dist.] 1981); *Hernandez v. State*, 914 S.W.2d 218 (Tex. App.- El Paso 1996) for examples of cases involving claims of defense of property. Notice how the facts behind a defense of property claim can also involve self-defense.
>
> Watch the news for stories about self-defense and defense of property cases. The D.A. decides which cases are submitted to a Grand Jury. Notice which cases are true billed by a Grand Jury.

SANCTIONED USES OF FORCE

In addition to defining the right of self-defense and defense of property, Chapter 9 of the Penal Code defines situations in which the use of force is lawful as long as the person using force reasonably believes it is necessary and does not use more than is necessary:

- Section 9.51 sanctions the use of force by a peace officer when it is reasonably necessary to make an arrest or conduct a search. Deadly force is justified when the officer reasonably believes the conduct for which an arrest is authorized involved the use or attempted use of deadly force or the officer reasonably believes there is a substantial risk that the arrestee will cause death or serious bodily injury to the officer or another person if the arrest is delayed.
- Section 9.52 provides that the use of force including deadly force is justified to prevent the escape of an arrested person from custody.
- Section 9.61 provides that the use of non-deadly force against a child less than 18 years old is justified by the child's parent or someone acting in loco parentis in order to discipline the child or promote his welfare.
- Section 9.62 allows for the use of non-deadly force by persons having the care and supervision of a child for a special purpose or to maintain discipline, most notably teachers.
- Section 9.63 permits persons who care for the mentally incompetent to use non-deadly force if it is necessary to promote the incompetent person's welfare, or if he is in an institution, to maintain discipline.

THE NECESSITY OR CHOICE OF EVILS DEFENSE

When the Texas legislature revised the Penal Code in 1974, it included a specific provision recognizing the general necessity defense. Prior to 1974, Texas recognized the principle of the necessity defense in special, limited statutes: allowing abortion to save a mother's life, destruction of a house to save another house from fire and speeding for police, fire and emergency vehicles.

The 1974 statute was codified in section 9.22 of the T.P.C. and is largely based on the Model Penal Code statute. It provides that conduct is justified if:

- the defendant reasonably believes it is immediately necessary to avoid imminent harm;
- according to ordinary standards of reasonableness, the desirability and urgency of avoiding the harm clearly outweigh the harm sought to be prevented by the law prohibiting the conduct; and
- there is no apparent legislative purpose to exclude the justification for the conduct.

"Harm" is defined in section 1.07 of the Penal Code to mean "anything reasonably regarded as loss, disadvantage, or injury, including harm to another person in whose welfare the person affected is interested." There is generally no limit on the type of harm to be avoided. The harm to be avoided does not have to involve a personal threat to the individual claiming the necessity defense. The statute does not place a limit on the magnitude of the harm to be avoided. The law anticipates a balancing between the harm caused by the offense and the harm the defendant was trying to escape. Texas courts have refused to recognize the defense in situations involving political protest, such as abortion clinic demonstrations that have led to disorderly conduct charges or campus demonstrations against university policies.

The necessity defense in Texas is very broad. The law does not require that the defendant be guilt-free of contributing to the emergency causing him to face a choice in order to claim the defense. It also does not deny the defense to defendants whose choices were based on reasonable and honest mistakes. Unlike some states, Texas does not limit the defense to only certain crimes. Even the offense of murder can be justified under the necessity defense.

In *Bush v. State*, 624 S.W.2d 377 (Tex. App. - Dallas 1981), the appellate court refused to allow the necessity defense to a woman who was convicted of driving while intoxicated. She argued that she feared her husband would physically harm her, and she had to leave the scene. Unfortunately, after she stopped for 15 minutes at her place of employment, she got on the road again. The court concluded that Bush failed to show that her conduct was reasonably necessary to avoid imminent harm.

In *Johnson v. State*, 650 S.W.2d 414 (Tex Crim. App. 1983), the Court of Criminal Appeals was faced with the claim that Johnson was justified in unlawfully carrying a weapon because he was in a high crime area. The court refused the necessity defense, finding that merely being in a high crime area does not constitute a reasonable belief that carrying a weapon is necessary to avoid imminent harm. On the other hand, in *Vasquez v. State*, 830 S.W.2d 948 (Tex Crim. App. 1992), the Court of Criminal Appeals ruled that unlawfully carrying a weapon may be justified under the necessity defense because the appellant was a former state prisoner who was in danger from other ex-inmates in the freeworld. There was evidence he had been attacked by former prisoners in a prison gang-related vendetta. In *Armstrong v. State*, 653 S.W.2d 810 (Tex Crim. App. 1983), Armstrong had been raped two weeks before being arrested for illegally carrying a handgun. The rapist threatened her with death if she reported the crime and had been harassing her. The court ruled that the jury should have been permitted to evaluate her necessity defense.

Exercises:
Did the necessity defense work for Ronald Bell in *Bell v. State*, 885 S.W.2d 282 (Tex. App. - Beaumont 1994). Bell claimed that he smoked marijuana because it relieved his stress and curbed his desire for alcohol.

Wilson claimed necessity justified his escape from prison to seek aid from his attorney and to get relief from sordid prison conditions. See *Wilson v. State*, 777 S.W.2d 823 (Tex. App. - Austin 1989).

FINAL THOUGHTS ON JUSTIFICATION DEFENSES

The law makes it difficult to justify the commission of a crime for a good reason. Violence should be discouraged. Individuals should seek peaceful, non-violent resolutions to their conflicts. They should seek legal ways of resolving difficult situations. Nonetheless, self-defense and defense of property are often raised in criminal cases. A lot of violent crimes involve people who know each other. The facts get complicated. It is a close call as to who provoked whom, who attacked first, was more force used than was necessary to protect oneself, was the danger immediate. Juries are asked to ferret through conflicting evidence and make judgments that deeply affect the lives of defendants and victims. Juries reflect evolving social standards.

We have come a long way from the Wild West and vigilante justice. Progress has been slow, however, because the decisions are not easy and we can all imagine the need to defend our loved ones or ourselves. Justification defenses strike us at a gut level.

MULTIPLE CHOICE QUESTIONS

1. Jimmy was at the wrong place at the wrong time. As he was leaving the apartment of his fellow law school buddy, the police knocked down the door and ordered everyone to lie on the floor. Jimmy's buddy, unbeknownst to him, turned out to be a drug dealer. The police were asking few questions. Without search warrants or arrest warrants, they hauled Jimmy and his friend down to the station. Jimmy figured it was an illegal arrest and reviewed his options:

    a. Jimmy had the right to resist the officers with force because it was an unlawful arrest.
    b. Jimmy had the right to resist the officer because he was innocent.
    c. Both a and b
    d. Jimmy had no right to use force to resist the officers unless they used more force than was necessary to arrest him and Jimmy needed to protect himself.

2. Sid decided to pick a fight with Lloyd. Unfortunately for Sid, Lloyd was a black belt in karate. Sid was losing and held up a white handkerchief in surrender, yelling, "I quit, you win." Lloyd kept chopping away, ignoring the signs of surrender. Sid was forced to keep fighting. Lloyd argued at trial that Sid provoked the fight:

    a. Sid cannot argue self-defense because he started it.
    b. Sid cannot argue self-defense because he should have tried to leave the scene in an obvious retreat.
    c. Sid can argue that he tried to abandon the encounter and continued the fight in self-defense.
    d. Sid can argue self-defense if he first tried to talk through his disagreement with Lloyd.

3. Barbara was sitting home reading a book and watching one of the weeknight magazine shows of which she is so fond. She heard someone at her backdoor and grabbed her revolver. She went to the door and ascertained that someone was trying to break in. She shot and killed the perpetrator. Barbara argues she was justified:

    a. Her defense will not be successful because the perpetrator was not yet in her home.
    b. She can argue self-defense and defense of property.
    c. She has a good self-defense claim, but no claim of defense of property.
    d. She can claim defense of property if she can show that she reasonably believed the perpetrator was armed.

4. In Texas, a person can carry a weapon when they visit their rival about their various disagreements, without jeopardizing their claim of self-defense in the event things did not go well:

    a. True
    b. False

5. Deadly force can be used in defense of property:

   a. only when the property is very valuable and can never be replaced.
   b. to prevent a person from the immediate commission of arson, burglary, robbery, aggravated robbery, theft or criminal mischief during the nighttime.
   c. there is never an occasion when deadly force can be used, only non-deadly force can be used to protect property.
   d. only if a sign is posted warning that deadly force will be used.

6. Jimmy was so angry with Sid because of his arrest while at Sid's house that he decided to get even. Since he did not want to destroy his chances of being a successful lawyer some day, Jimmy decided against the use of physical violence. Instead, upon Sid's release on bail, Jimmy went to Sid's house one evening and slit the tires on Sid's classic Mustang convertible, which was parked in the driveway out front. Sid heard someone outside and retrieved his revolver. He opened the door just as Jimmy was running away from the scene and saw the damage to his car. Sid shot and killed Jimmy.

   a. Sid can claim defense of his property because Jimmy was committing criminal mischief at nighttime.
   b. Sid can claim self-defense because Jimmy was committing burglary.
   c. Sid cannot claim self-defense because the criminal mischief had already been completed and Jimmy was fleeing the scene.
   d. Sid cannot claim self-defense because he provoked Jimmy into getting even with him.

7. Barbara decided to put up an electric fence around her home that would cause serious bodily injury to anyone who crossed it. Such a device is:

   a. legal in Texas.
   b. illegal in Texas because it is designed to cause serious harm.
   c. legal if Barbara posts a warning sign.
   d. illegal because such devices are never allowed, no matter how much harm they cause.

8. Mr. Smith could not afford his wife's medication, which was necessary to save her life, and burglarized a pharmacy to steal some for her. He argues the defense of necessity:

   a. Mr. Smith will succeed in his defense because the theft was a lesser evil than his wife's death.
   b. Mr. Smith will not succeed in his defense because economic necessity has not been recognized by the courts as a valid use of the necessity defense.
   c. Mr. Smith will only succeed if he can show that there was no other way for him to procure the medication.
   d. Mr. Smith will not succeed because Texas does not recognize the defense.

9. Your mother requested that you watch her house and yard while she was touring the world. You visited her home daily and did a thorough check to make sure things were going well. During one of your daytime visits, you noticed a prowler lurking in the backyard, which was not fenced in, walking off with the patio furniture. You ran after him with your baseball bat and knocked him in the head. He lives:

    a. You can argue that you were permitted you were permitted to use force because your mother had requested your help.
    b. You can argue that you were defending yourself because you did not know what the prowler would do if he saw you.
    c. You cannot use force to defend someone else's property. You should have called the police.
    d. You cannot use what might have been deadly force to protect your mother's property.

10. The same scenario as Question 9, only the prowler died as a result of your powerful blow:

    a. You were justified because you could have used the same deadly force to protect your own property. The prowler was committing theft.
    b. You were justified because there was no other way to recover the property.
    c. You were not justified because the prowler was committing his crime during the daytime.
    d. You were not justified because deadly force to protect a third party's property is never allowed. Call the police!!

CHAPTER EIGHT

DEFENSES TO CRIMINAL LIABILITY: EXCUSES

INTRODUCTION

Unlike justification defenses to criminal liability, excuse defenses do not claim that the defendant had the right to engage in behavior that under other circumstances would be considered criminal. Excuse defenses claim that for certain clearly established legal reasons, the defendant's actions should be excused. Just as with the justification defenses discussed in Chapter Seven, the defendant must introduce sufficient evidence at trial to establish that the jury should be instructed to consider the excuse defense during its deliberations. This chapter will focus on several excuse defenses as defined by Texas law:

(1) the insanity defense;
(2) mistake of law and mistake of fact defenses;
(3) intoxication;
(4) duress;
(5) entrapment; and
(6) age.

There are significant differences among state and federal penal codes in the area of excuse defenses. Like justification defenses, excuse defenses are controversial and have been the subject of significant public debate. In recent years state legislatures have been active in revamping insanity and entrapment defenses. There is considerable disagreement concerning the age at which individuals should be held responsible for their crimes in the adult criminal justice system. As you read the Texas statutes and case law, anticipate the future direction this area of law might go.

THE INSANITY DEFENSE

Insanity in Texas is an affirmative defense, according to section 2.04 of the T.P.C., which means the burden of persuasion is on the defendant to convince the jury of his claim by a preponderance of the evidence. There is no legal presumption that a defendant was sane at the time of the offense. As an affirmative defense, the defendant has both the burden of initially raising the defense and the burden of proving it by a preponderance of the evidence. Texas has adopted a strict M'Naghton insanity defense, defined by section 8.01(a):

It is an affirmative defense to prosecution that, at the time of the conduct charged, the actor, as a result of severe mental disease or defect, did not know that his conduct was wrong.

Prior to 1983, section 8.01 also included an "irresistible impulse" test. It provided that if because of mental disease or defect, the accused did not know his conduct was wrong <u>or was unable to conform his behavior to the law</u>, he was entitled to be acquitted on the basis of insanity. In 1983, the Texas legislature considered abolishing the defense entirely but decided against it after similar efforts failed for constitutional reasons in Florida, Wyoming, and Arizona. Instead, the legislature abolished the irresistible impulse test. The Texas Family Code, section 55.05, continues to use the pre-1983 insanity standard with respect to juvenile offenders.

The issue of insanity is not strictly medical. It also generates both legal and ethical considerations. Texas courts have said that in deciding the ultimate issue of sanity, only the jury can bring together the non-medical components that must be considered to reach a final outcome. Otherwise, insanity would be decided in the hospitals and not in the courtrooms. One may be suffer from a mental disease or defect and not be legally exonerated for criminal acts. Stated the Texas Court of Criminal Appeals in *Graham v. State*, 566 S.W.2d 941, 952 (Tex. Crim. App. 1978):

> Ultimately the issue of insanity at the time of the offense excusing criminal responsibility lies in the province of the jury, not only as to the credibility of the witnesses and the weight of the evidence, but also as to the limits of the defense itself.

If an insanity defense is submitted to the jury, there are three possible verdicts: guilty, not guilty, or not guilty by reason of insanity. A defendant found not guilty by reason of insanity is acquitted of the offense. Under the Texas Code of Criminal Procedure, article 46.03, section 1(e), jurors are not permitted to have information about the legal meaning of the not guilty by reason of insanity verdict. They are not told what happens after such a verdict is rendered. The underlying notion of this restriction is once a jury decides to find a person not guilty by reason of insanity, its responsibility ends. The consequences of the verdict are not the jurors' concern. This provision of the Code of Criminal Procedure is different from provisions in several other jurisdictions where the defendant can request that the jury be informed about what happens after an insanity verdict is rendered. In those jurisdictions, jurors are advised about the civil commitment proceedings that follow such a verdict.

Expert Testimony

Even though the jury has the final say on the issue of insanity, mental health experts play a pivotal role in the adversarial system. Both the defendant and the State can call experts to testify about the defendant's mental health and his or her ability to know right from wrong. Psychiatrists not only present testimony, they help to determine before trial whether the insanity defense is viable and assist in preparing cross-examination of the other side's psychiatric expert. Because psychiatry is not an exact science, equally competent practitioners confronted with the same information often disagree in their diagnoses in an area that is complex and strange to lawyers and jurors alike.

An indigent defendant needs a psychiatrist as much as someone who can afford to retain one. The Texas Court of Criminal Appeals ruled in *De Freece v. State*, 848 S.W.2d 150 (Tex. Crim. App. 1993) that under the Texas Code of Criminal Procedure due process requires that indigent defendants are appointed a competent psychiatrist to provide technical assistance, help evaluate the strength of the defense, identify the weakness in the State's case, and testify and/or prepare counsel to cross-examine the opposing experts. The defendant is not entitled to a psychiatrist of his choice, or even one who believes he was insane at the time of the crime. Under the Texas Code of Criminal Procedure, the trial judge can also appoint a disinterested expert to examine the defendant with regard to the insanity defense. The appointment of a neutral expert, however, does not negate the defendant's right to have an expert appointed on his behalf.

Although experts are generally involved in insanity cases, the law is clear that lay witnesses can recount germane observations of a defendant and give an opinion on the defendant's sanity. In fact, lay opinion testimony alone can support a finding of insanity. In the same vein, if a defendant presents expert testimony on the insanity issue, the State does not have to counter with an expert. The State can counter with lay testimony, and the jury can reject the psychiatric testimony based on the lay testimony. In *Morris v. State*, 744 S.W.2d 290 (Tex. App. - Corpus Christi 1987), Morris offered the testimony of several mental health experts about his ability to know right from wrong as a result of a mental disease. The State offered the testimony of several police officers who observed Morris and several other persons who knew him. They all testified that in their opinion Morris was sane, and he was convicted. Morris argued that the jury's verdict was against the weight of the evidence, but he lost his appeal.

Mental Disease or Defect

Section 8.01(b) of the Penal Code provides that the term "mental disease or defect" does not include an abnormality manifested only by repeated criminal or otherwise antisocial conduct. In other words, a defendant cannot prove insanity by presenting evidence of nothing other than repeated criminal acts and other antisocial behavior.

An argument introducing a variation of the 8.01(b) provision is found in *Sanders v. State*, 604 S.W.2d 108 (Tex. Crim. App. 1980), in which Sanders plead insanity to a charge of murder. Four psychiatrists and a psychologist testified that he had been seriously mentally ill since 1970 and did not know right from wrong. The State tried to introduce evidence about a murder Sanders committed in 1970 for which he had been found not guilty by reason of insanity. The State's theory was that based on his prior experience, the appellant knew that he could plead insanity and be acquitted. The court refused to allow evidence of his prior insanity acquittal to be introduced because it was not relevant to his current offense.

The question of whose moral code should be used to determine whether a defendant knew right from wrong was at issue in *Bigby v. State*, 892 S.W.2d 864 (Tex. Crim. App. 1994). Bigby murdered his friend and co-worker and his friend's son. There was conflicting expert evidence about Bigby's mental state and the seriousness of his mental disorder at the time of the offense. When the police arrested him, Bigby admitted he was guilty of the murders. Several experts testified that in their opinion, Bigby knew his conduct was illegal, but he did not know it was morally wrong. The court decided that focusing on Bigby's moral beliefs was incorrect.

The question of insanity should focus on whether a defendant understood the nature and quality of his action and whether it was an act he ought to do. By accepting and acknowledging that his behavior was illegal by society's standards, Bigby understood that others believed his conduct was wrong.

In *Beasely v. State*, 810 S.W.2d 838 (Tex. App. -Ft. Worth 1991), Janis Beasely was arrested for driving while intoxicated. She argued that she was diagnosed as manic-depressive and was taking medication for her condition. On the evening of her arrest she had run out of her medication and was suffering from a trance-like state. She appealed her conviction because the trial judge refused to allow the jury to consider an insanity defense. The Court of Appeals ruled that because driving while intoxicated is a strict liability crime that does not require a culpable mental state, a defendant could not plead insanity.

Exercises:

We tend to associate the insanity defense with murder charges. Read *Barnett v. State*, 771 S.W.2d 654 (Tex. App. - Corpus Christi 1989). Barnett was convicted of the unauthorized use of a motor vehicle. The jury rejected his insanity plea even though an expert testified that in his opinion Barnett was insane on the day of the offense.

In *Taylor v. State,* 856 S.W.2d 459 (Tex. App. -Houston [1st Dist.] 1993), the appellant was convicted of murdering her four-year old daughter. The evidence showed that Valerie Taylor had significant mental problems that led to paranoid delusions, including the delusion that her daughter was trying to kill her infant brother. Taylor stabbed the little girl over 20 times. The two psychiatrists who testified at trial reached different conclusions as to Taylor's sanity. Several lay persons who knew Taylor testified about her sanity as well. Read the case and see why you think the jury concluded that Taylor was not insane and why the appellate court did not reverse the jury verdict.

Marie Olivier was convicted of murder. The evidence showed she had been institutionalized numerous times for mental illness, had been in psychotherapy since high school, received electric shock treatments, and was in a psychiatric hospital a few days before the offense. Before the murder, she was taking Elavil and Vicodin but stopped taking them after a religious group influenced her. Olivier left the hospital a few days before the murder and met with the religious group to pray for healing and to cast out Satan. For several days she wandered throughout the city of Houston preaching to street people. She killed her 14-month old child because, as she testified, she thought her daughter was Satan. Three psychiatrists testified at trial that Marie was insane at the time of the murder and did not know right from wrong. The State argued that the appellant was faking her mental illness. The State presented no expert testimony. The Court of Appeals reversed the jury's decision, finding the verdict manifestly unjust. *Olivier v. State*, 850 S.W.2d 742 (Tex. App. - Houston [14th Dist.] 1993).

Competency to Stand Trial

The insanity defense is different from a decision that a defendant is incompetent to stand trial. Competency addresses the defendant's ability to consult with his lawyer with a reasonable degree of rational understanding concerning the proceedings against him. The issue of competency is resolved in advance of a guilt/innocence trial on a motion from the defendant. In Texas, a jury decides whether there is sufficient evidence that a defendant is incompetent. The jury that decides competency cannot determine guilt or innocence. The burden of production and persuasion is on the defendant, and proof must be established by a preponderance of the evidence. A finding of incompetency to stand trial does not mean that the defendant was legally insane at the time of the offense. The insanity defense focuses on the defendant's ability to know that his behavior was wrong. The competency question focuses on his ability to assist in his criminal defense. The law of competency to stand trial is found in the Texas Code of Criminal Procedure, article 46.02.

MISTAKE OF FACT

Section 8.02 of the T.P.C. provides that it is a defense to prosecution that the defendant, because of a mistake, formed a reasonable belief regarding a fact, if his mistaken belief negated the culpable mental state required for the commission of the crime. A reasonable belief means a belief that would be held by an ordinary and prudent person in the same circumstances as the defendant. Mistake of fact is a defense as opposed to an affirmative defense. As explained in section 2.03 of the T.P.C., this means that a reasonable doubt on the issue requires that the defendant be acquitted.

The defense was raised in *Wages v. State*, 703 S.W.2d 736 (Tex. App. - Houston [14th Dist.] 1985). In that case, Donna Wages was convicted of writing bad checks. The testimony showed she and her husband were small business owners, and he wrote several insufficient fund checks to her on the business account that she cashed. Her husband testified that his wife did not know the financial status of the business and that the checks were worthless. He intentionally kept his wife in the dark. The court refused Donna Wages' request for a mistake of fact jury instruction because there was nothing in evidence, other than her husband's testimony, that she was unaware of the worthless checks. She did not testify at trial so there was no evidence of what she believed to be the facts. In addition, there was evidence that the business received many bank notices about the dishonored checks. The question was raised as to whether a reasonable person would have believed there was sufficient money in the business bank account to cover the checks made payable to Ms. Wages.

Exercise:
Alberta Beggs was convicted of injury to a child under section 22.04 of the T.P.C. She argued on appeal that the jury should have been provided a mistake of fact instruction. She and her stepdaughter were charged with burning her granddaughter in hot bath water. Beggs admitted to helping her stepdaughter punish her granddaughter by administering the bath that scolded the child. Her defense was that she did not know that the bath water was hot enough to cause injury. Her stepdaughter had drawn the water before she came into the bathroom to help bathe the child. She thought the water temperature was normal because the child hated to bathe and a normal bath would have been punishment to her. How do you think the Court of Criminal Appeals ruled concerning the instruction? See *Beggs v. State*, 597 S.W.2d 375 (Tex. Crim. App. 1980).

MISTAKE OF LAW

Section 8.03 of the T.P.C. provides that ignorance of the law is no defense to prosecution. It is an affirmative defense, however, if the defendant reasonably believed his conduct was not a crime based upon a written, official statement of the law from an administrative agency or public official charged with the responsibility for interpreting the law, or a written opinion of a court of record interpreting the law.

The mistake of law defense was raised by Richard Gallegos who was convicted of bail jumping and failing to appear in *Gallegos v. State*, 828 S.W.2d 577 (Tex. App. - Houston [1st Dist.] 1992). He had appealed his Texas conviction for possession of marijuana. According to the terms of his appeal bond, he was permitted to live in Louisiana, but in the event his appeal was affirmed, he was required to return to Chambers County, Texas. Gallegos's conviction was affirmed, but he failed to appear at a court setting. His excuse for missing the hearing was that his Louisiana attorney advised him not to appear. The Texas Court of Appeals ruled that Gallegos was not entitled to a mistake of law defense because his decision not to return was not based on an official statement or interpretation of law by a court or an administrative agency. The court also ruled he was not entitled to argue mistake of fact, stating that a defendant who relied on another's mistake of law cannot claim a mistake of fact.

INTOXICATION

According to section 8.04 of the T.P.C., voluntary intoxication cannot serve as a defense to a criminal charge. Intoxication includes any impairment of mental or physical capacity that results from the introduction of any substance into the body. Intoxication is voluntary if the defendant exercised independent judgment or will in taking the intoxicant. Any substance, both legal and illegal in nature can cause intoxication. Although voluntary intoxication is not a defense to a crime, it may be relevant to the defendant's mens rea. It may also be relevant to show the defendant did not possess a required level of skill or physical ability to perform the crime charged against him.

Section 8.04 also provides that the defendant can introduce evidence of temporary insanity caused by intoxication in mitigation of the penalty attached to the offense. The Texas courts have ruled that proof of temporary insanity as the result of intoxication must be read in conjunction with section 8.01 of the T.P.C. concerning the insanity defense. This means that in order to obtain a mitigation instruction for the jury because of voluntary intoxication, there must be evidence that, as a result of intoxication at the time the crime was committed, the defendant did not know his conduct was wrong.

In *Joiner v. State*, 814 S.W.2d 135 (Tex. App. - Houston [14th Dist.] 1991), the defendant was convicted of injury to a 13-year old girl who he attempted to attack sexually. When she resisted his advances, he beat her. He claimed that he had been drinking and taking L.S.D. throughout the day, and the child, who was the daughter of his friend, reminded him of his mother when she was intoxicated. He became angry and attacked the girl. The court ruled that Joiner was not entitled to a jury charge about temporary insanity as a result of intoxication because there was no evidence that he did not know right from wrong.

Although involuntary intoxication is not recognized as a defense in the Texas Penal Code, Texas courts have recognized it as a defense when it is established that the defendant exercised no independent will or judgment in taking the intoxicant. Helen Torres was convicted of aggravated robbery. She contended that at the time of the crime she was involuntarily intoxicated. Helen and Robert Miranda broke into the victim's house, held her at gun point, stole her property, forced her to accompany them to her bank and cash several checks made payable to them. At the bank, the victim was able to notify the security officer that something was wrong, and the two robbers were apprehended after an exchange of gunfire.

Miranda testified at Torres's trial that he had slipped thorazine tablets into an alka selzer drink he prepared for her because she felt sick. The Texas Court of Criminal Appeals ruled in *Torres v. State*, 585 S.W.2d 748 (Tex. Crim. App. 1979), that involuntary intoxication is a defense in Texas even though it is not mentioned in the Penal Code. The insanity defense under section 8.01 also applies to involuntary intoxication: as a result of being involuntarily intoxicated, the defendant did not know her conduct was wrong or was unable to conform her conduct to the requirements of the law (*Torres* was decided prior to the change in the insanity defense in 1983). The court ruled that Helen Torres was entitled to a jury instruction on involuntary intoxication.

In another case, *Hanks v. State*, 542 S.W.2d 413 (Tex. Crim. App. 1978), the court ruled that a defendant can not rely on involuntary intoxication as a defense if he suspected that he was being subjected to an intoxicant but consumed it anyway. Evidence that the defendant was an alcoholic also will not raise the defense of involuntary intoxication. *Watson v. State*, 654 S.W.2d 730 (Tex. App. - Houston [14th Dist.] 1983).

DURESS

In section 8.05 of the Texas, it is an affirmative defense to prosecution in a felony case that the defendant committed the crime because he was compelled to do so by threat of imminent death or serious bodily injury to himself or another. In a prosecution for a misdemeanor crime, it is an affirmative defense that the defendant committed the crime because he was compelled to do so by force or the threat of force. Texas makes a distinction between the amount of force that can be relied on to argue duress in a felony case and the amount of force that can be relied on for the duress defense to a misdemeanor. The duress defense can be used even against murder charges.

An objective or reasonable person test is used to determine whether the requisite compulsion existed. Under section 8.05(c), compulsion exists only if the threat would have rendered a person of reasonable firmness incapable of resisting the pressure. If the defendant intentionally, knowingly, or recklessly placed himself in a situation in which it was probable he would be subjected to compulsion, the defense is not available. Finally, acting merely at the command of a spouse is no defense, unless the defendant acted under the kind of compulsion that would satisfy 8.05(c).

> **Exercises:**
> Criminal defendants can argue more than one legal theory in their defense. The same facts can provide the groundwork for both the necessity defense and the duress defense. Spakes was convicted of escape when he fled the county jail with three other inmates. He claimed he escaped under threat from the other inmates. If he told authorities about the escape or refused to go with them, he would be killed. Both duress and necessity were issues in the case. *Spakes v. State*, 891 S.W.2d 7 (Tex. App. - Amarillo 1994).
>
> David Montgomery was a narcotics informant. He was convicted of aggravated robbery, but claimed both a mistake of fact because he did not know the person he was working with was not a police officer and duress because he cooperated with the police out of fear of reprisal. The court discussed the submission of more than one legal defense for the jury to consider based on the same facts. See *Montgomery v. State*, 588 S.W.2d 950 (Tex. Crim. App. 1979).

ENTRAPMENT

Section 8.06 of the Penal Code provides that it is a defense to prosecution that the defendant committed a crime as a result of being induced by law enforcement agents using persuasion or other means likely to cause the defendant's conduct. Entrapment is not available if the agent's behavior merely provided the defendant with the opportunity to commit a crime. "Law enforcement agent" means any personnel of local, state, or federal law enforcement agencies and any persons acting pursuant to their instructions. As a defense, the prosecution must persuade the jury that it did not exist beyond a reasonable doubt.

In 1994, the Texas Court of Criminal Appeals significantly changed the test of entrapment in Texas in a 5-4 en banc decision, *England v. State*, 887 S.w.2d 902 (Tex. Crim. App. 1994). Prior to *England*, the court had decided that the Texas legislature had enacted a purely objective test for entrapment. Once the defendant showed that he had been the target of persuasive police conduct, regardless of whether he was actually persuaded to commit the offense by the police behavior, the court's focus was directed to the police conduct. The question was whether the persuasion used by the law enforcement agent was such as to cause a hypothetical person - an ordinary law abiding person of average resistance - to commit the crime. There was no need to examine the defendant's proclivities or predisposition to engage in criminal activity. The defendant's prior criminal history or reputation was not admissible unless it went to the issue of whether the police had used persuasion versus provided the defendant with an opportunity.

The *England* court reanalyzed the entrapment defense and the wording of section 8.06. It determined that the legislature actually enacted a mixed objective/subjective test for entrapment. On the subjective side of the mixed test, a defendant must produce evidence that he was actually induced to commit the crime because of police conduct. Evidence of predisposition and prior criminal history is relevant to the issue of whether the defendant was induced by law enforcement or whether he was predisposed to engage in crime. The objective part of the standard still requires the defendant prove that the police used such persuasion as to induce a hypothetical person of ordinary law abiding nature to commit the offense.

England demonstrates how powerful courts are in defining the criminal law. Their interpretive powers can be as important as the wording of the statute itself. For many years, Texas used an objective standard for entrapment, based upon the court's understanding of section 8.06. In 1994, the same Texas court (obviously with different judges), interpreting the same statute, decided that the state legislature had meant something quite different. The case is also interesting because the court's opinion reviews the federal and Model Penal Code entrapment standard and discusses the status of the law in other jurisdictions.

Exercises:
For interesting cases that show situations in which entrapment is raised as a defense: *January v. State*, 720 S.W.2d 207 (Tex. App. - Houston [14th Dist.] 1986); *Ramos v. State*, 632 S.W.2d 688 (Tex. App. - Amarillo 1982); *Rodriguez v. State*, 819 S.W.2d 654 (Tex. App. - Fort Worth 1991); *Lopez V. State*, 824 S.W.2d 298 (Tex. App. - Houston [14th Dist.] 1992).

Examples of cases in which law enforcement inducement was held sufficient: *Gifford v. State*, 740 S.W.2d 76 (Tex. App. - Fort Worth 1987) in which a false representation by the agent that the conduct was legal was considered entrapment as matter of law. *Gobin v. State*, 684 S.W.2d 802 (Tex. App. - Fort Worth 1985) in which the informant's threat to withhold rent money was considered inducement.

Examples of cases where law enforcement inducement was not held sufficient: *Sebesta v. State*, 783 S.W.2d 811 (Tex. App. - Houston [1st Dist.] 1990) held that annoying telephone calls by a government informant were not sufficient to cause a person to commit a crime. Economic circumstances cannot substitute for inducement. *Cardona v. State*, 768 S.W.2d 823 (Tex. App. - Houston [14th Dist.] 1989).

AGE

Can there be a more controversial topic than the age at which perpetrators of crime should be prosecuted as adults? As rates of violent juvenile crime rise, so does the intensity of the discussion. State legislatures throughout the country are revisiting their laws about adult responsibility for certain types of offenses. While everyone agrees there is still a need for a juvenile justice system, there are many voices advocating that the adult system is more appropriate for some young offenders who commit violent crimes.

Section 8.07(a) of the T.P.C. provides that a person cannot be convicted of a crime in an adult court if the crime was committed when the person was younger than 15 years old, with the exception of certain offenses:

- perjury and aggravated perjury when it is apparent he had sufficient understanding of the oath;
- traffic laws and ordinances other than driving while intoxicated;
- misdemeanors punishable by fine only, except public intoxication;
- violations of penal ordinances of political subdivisions;

- violations of penal statutes that are, or are less included offenses of, a capital felony, an aggravated controlled substance felony, or a felony of the first degree if the person committed the offense when 14 years of age or older and for which the person is transferred for prosecution to the court under Section 54.02 of the Texas Family Code.

For a clear reading of section 8.07, it must be read in conjunction with Section 54.02 of the Family Code. A juvenile older than 15 and younger than 17 cannot be prosecuted in an adult criminal court for any offenses except those listed in section 8.07(a). The juvenile court can waive jurisdiction and certify a 14 to 17 year old for prosecution in the adult courts pursuant to Section 54.02 of the Texas Family Code in the event the child committed a capital felony, an aggravated controlled substance felony, or a felony of the first degree. A child between 15 and 17 years old can be transferred to the adult system if he committed a felony of the second or third degree or a state jail felony.

The procedures for waiving jurisdiction to an adult court are found in Chapter 54 of the Family Code. In addition to making certain that the child is of the correct age to be transferred and that he or she has committed a transferable offense, the Family Court is mandated by section 54.01 to look at:

- whether the offense was committed against a person or property;
- whether the offense was committed in an aggressive and premeditated manner;
- whether there is evidence on which a grand jury could indict;
- the child's sophistication and maturity;
- the record and previous history of the child; and
- prospects for protecting the public and the likelihood of the child's rehabilitation in the juvenile justice system.

Although the United States Supreme Court ruled that the death penalty could not be enforced against any person found guilty of a crime committed under the age of 16, section 8.07(c) of the T.P.C. states that no person can be executed for a crime committed under 17.

FINAL COMMENTS ON EXCUSE DEFENSES

Although excuse defenses raise a lot of public criticism, they are seldom successful. Like many states, Texas has tightened the range of behaviors for which the excuse defenses are available. A stricter insanity defense was legislated in 1983 with the elimination of the irresistible impulse test. In 1994, the Texas Court of Criminal Appeals created a more difficult entrapment defense by introducing a subjective component to a previously objective standard. Effective 1996, youths as young as 14 year old who commit certain serious offenses became eligible for transfer to the adult criminal court system, a reduction from the age of 15. Time will determine whether more changes are in the offing.

MULTIPLE CHOICE QUESTIONS

1. Henry spent the evening drinking martinis and snorting cocaine. Sometime during the early morning, he stopped at a convenience store to purchase cigarettes. The clerk had had a bad night and was rude to Henry who he suspected was intoxicated. Henry pulled out his handgun and shot the clerk dead. Henry has no previous criminal history and argued temporary insanity as a result of intoxication. To argue that defense successfully in Texas, Henry must:

    a. establish that he was intoxicated involuntarily.
    b. establish that he was not a chronic substance abuser.
    c. establish that he did not know the nature of his actions or right from wrong.
    d. establish that he tried to reason with the clerk before he shot him.

2. Harriet sold drugs to an undercover law enforcement officer after he begged and pleaded, saying that if he did not get the drugs he was going to commit suicide. Harriet and he had been "dating" for several months. Harriet pled entrapment. Under the Texas test, Harriet must show:

    a. that the officer's persuasion would have induced a hypothetical law abiding person to sell him drugs.
    b. that the officer's persuasion actually induced her to sell him drugs.
    c. that Harriet had never sold drugs before.
    d. a and b

3. Harriet was a drug dealer before she sold the drugs to the undercover officer; however, she had turned over a new leaf and for eight months had been out of the drug selling business. Is that relevant evidence in Texas to her entrapment defense?

    a. Yes, because it goes to whether Harriet was actually induced by the officer's pleas.
    b. No, because the entrapment test is only concerned with the officer's behavior.
    c. No, because Harriet's prior history is not admissible.
    d. Yes, because it shows Harriet was a changed woman.

4. Insanity in Texas must be proved by the defendant beyond a reasonable doubt.

    a. True
    b. False

5. The Texas entrapment defense is:

    a. an objective test.
    b. a subjective test.
    c. a mixed objective/subjective test.
    d. the law is not clear.

6. Involuntary intoxication is a defense to criminal prosecution defined in section 8.04 of the Penal Code.

    a. True
    b. False

7. Duress or coercion in Texas can only be pled for nonviolent felony cases.

    a. True
    b. False

8. Joey was 14 ½ years old when he recklessly caused the death of another individual as a result of running over his neighbor with his skateboard. The neighbor was a healthy 23-year-old woman who fell to the ground and suffered a concussion to her head. Joey had been in juvenile court for several other skateboard-related accidents, none of which, however, had led to a death. The D.A. was considering petitioning the Family Court to transfer Joey to the adult court. Is this possible?

    a. Yes, Joey was over 14 and can be certified as an adult.
    b. Yes, Joey's prior juvenile history allows the D.A. to petition for transfer.
    c. No, Joey has to be facing at least a first-degree felony to be transferred.
    d. No, because no juvenile under 15 can be transferred to the adult courts in Texas.

9. Texas law requires that the defendant, who wants the judge to issue a jury instruction on the issue of insanity, must put into evidence testimony from a mental health expert.

    a. True
    b. False

10. The Texas courts have ruled that the prosecution must counter evidence of a defendant's insanity with expert testimony from a mental health practitioner to the effect that the defendant was sane because lay testimony is not sufficient.

    a. True
    b. False

CHAPTER NINE

CRIMES AGAINST PERSONS: CRIMINAL HOMICIDE

INTRODUCTION

Murder cases intrigue us. They get more media coverage than other types of crimes, and murder is the favorite topic of television crime dramas and mystery novels. Murder statutes have a higher public profile than other criminal statutes, especially in those states that have the death penalty. This chapter examines the Texas murder statute with a special emphasis on capital punishment. Texas receives national and international recognition because of its generous use of the death penalty. It is especially important that any discussion about murder in this state spend substantial time on understanding how capital punishment law has developed and why. Because Texas death penalty law is very different than death penalty law in any other jurisdictions, it is even more important to look at it. Could these differences explain why Texas sends more people to death row than any other state? Obviously, there are many contributing factors, but perhaps one factor is the unique Texas death penalty statute.

THE MURDER STATUTE

Texas no longer uses the first and second-degree murder scheme. Its murder statute is found in Chapter 19 of the Texas Penal Code and is based largely on the Model Penal Code. A person commits murder under section 19.01(b) if he:

1) intentionally or knowingly causes the death of another individual;
2) intends to cause serious bodily injury and commits an act clearly dangerous to human life that causes the death of an individual; or
3) commits or attempts to commit a felony, other than manslaughter, and in the course of an in furtherance of the commission or attempt, or in immediate flight from the commission or attempt, he commits or attempts to commit an act clearly dangerous to human life that causes death of an individual.

An offense under section 19.01 is a first-degree felony. "Individual" is defined in section 1.07 of the T.P.C. as a human being who has been born and is alive. There is no fetal death statute in Texas.

In 1993, the Texas legislature repealed the voluntary manslaughter statute that was located in section 19.04, and placed act of voluntary manslaughter into the murder statute, section 19.01. The traditional elements of voluntary manslaughter are now in 19.01(d):

At the punishment phase of the trial, the defendant may raise the issue as to whether he caused the death under the immediate influence of sudden passion arising from adequate cause. If the defendant proves the issue in the affirmative by a preponderance of the evidence, the offense is a felony of the second degree.

"Adequate cause" is defined in section 19.01(a)(1) as a cause that would commonly produce a degree of anger, rage, resentment, or terror in a person of ordinary temper, sufficient to render the mind incapable of cool reflection. "Sudden passion" is passion directly caused by and arising out of provocation by the victim or a person acting with the victim that arose at the time of the offense and is not solely the result of a former provocation. "A person of ordinary temper" is a reasonable person.

This means that voluntary manslaughter is no longer a separate homicide offense in Texas. It is considered a murder that can be reduced to a second-degree felony if the defendant introduces evidence that convinces the jury during the punishment phase by a preponderance of the evidence that he or she killed in sudden passion arising from adequate cause.

With the voluntary manslaughter statute repealed, what had previously been termed involuntary manslaughter was re-identified as manslaughter. It is a second-degree felony, defined in section 19.04 of the Penal Code as recklessly causing the death of an individual. "Criminally negligent homicide" is a separate offense defined by section 19.05 as causing the death of an individual by criminal negligence. It is punished as a state jail felony.

Murder Committed in the Heat of Passion and with Adequate Cause

Sudden passion arising from adequate cause are fact issues that a jury decides. Appellate courts are obviously reluctant to overturn a jury's decision on these issues if there was evidence to support its conclusion. An accused is entitled to a jury instruction on the issue of murder committed in the heat of passion if there was any evidence supporting it no matter how strong, weak, contradicted, unimpeached, or even unbelievable the evidence may be.

In *Perez v. State*, 940 S.W.2d 820 (Tex. App.- Waco 1997), the court ruled that the jury should have been instructed to consider the issue of provocation and sudden passion during the punishment phase. Perez offered evidence that showed he killed his friend during an argument. He suspected his friend was having an affair with his wife and believed that his friend carried a weapon. During the argument he saw his friend reach underneath his seat for something. Suspecting that he was reaching for a gun, Perez testified he became afraid and shot and killed the victim. His fear alone did not present evidence of killing in sudden passion, but if fear rendered him incapable of deliberate reflection, sudden passion could be argued. Perez had been convicted after first claiming self-defense during the guilt/innocence stage of his trial. The jury rejected that claim, after which Perez argued that he committed murder in the heat of passion. This case demonstrates how defendants can rely on more than one legal theory to prove their innocence or at least to mitigate their guilt. Depending on the facts, self-defense cases often combine heat of sudden passion arguments in a two-prong approach to the prosecution's case. It is easy to see how a self-defense claim can sometimes include facts that suggest the murder was committed with adequate cause.

> **Exercises:**
> In *Garza v. State*, 878 S.W.2d 213 (Tex. App. - Corpus Christi 1994), the defendant failed to convince the jury he had acted in sudden passion or provocation when he killed his estranged wife and a man she was talking to at a party where he saw them. What facts did the appellate court emphasize in their support of the jury?
>
> *Guerra v. State*, 936 S.W.2d 46 (Tex. App. - San Antonio 1996), involved another case where the defendant argued he was scared and emotionally excited when the victim threatened him with a knife. How did the court analyze Guerra's claims?

Reckless and Negligent Murders

The difference between the culpable mental states for manslaughter and criminally negligent homicide is the appreciation of the risk. Recklessness for a manslaughter charge requires proof that the defendant perceived the risk and disregarded it. In criminal negligence, the evidence must show the defendant did not perceive a risk that an ordinary person would have recognized.

> **Exercises:**
> Read *Vaughn & Sons, Inc. v. State*, 737 S.W.2d (Tex. Crim. App. 1987), concerning a corporation that was prosecuted for criminally negligent homicide. Vaughn, acting through two of its employees, caused the death of two individuals in a motor vehicle accident. A transport truck operated by Vaughn broke down and stalled in a moving lane of traffic. Approximately six hours later, during the nighttime, the victims crashed into the back of the truck, which was still in the traffic lane.
>
> In *Trepanier v. State*, 940 S.W.2d 827 (Tex. App. - Austin 1997), the appellant was convicted of manslaughter for killing a bicyclist while driving an automobile. The court refused to disrupt the jury's verdict that the appellant was reckless. Evidence showed the appellant was driving at an inappropriate speed in heavy traffic and attempted to pass a truck by driving on the shoulder of the road. The court concluded there was sufficient evidence that appellant voluntarily created a substantial and unjustifiable risk and consciously disregarded the risk of killing the bicyclist. The appellant argued he had a history of seizures and had forgotten to take his medication.
>
> The appellate court in *Saunders v. State*, 871 S.W.2d 920 (Tex. App. - Corpus Christi 1994), refused to rule the appellant was entitled to a jury instruction on negligent homicide. Saunders was convicted of murdering his girlfriend's five-month-old infant. Evidence showed the child died of injuries to the head caused by squeezing the infant's skull. There were other injuries from earlier traumas. Witnesses testified that they saw the appellant mistreat the infant on several occasions. The jury was instructed on the law of murder and manslaughter, but convicted him of murder. Saunders argued that the jury should have been instructed about negligent homicide.

CAPITAL PUNISHMENT: TEXAS STYLE

The Death Penalty Statute

In *Furman v. Georgia*, 408 U.S.238 (1972), the United States Supreme Court held that the Georgia death penalty statute violated the Eighth Amendment prohibition against cruel and unusual punishment. The *Furman* decision actually involved three separate cases that the Supreme Court consolidated into the *Furman* case. One of the other two cases also originated in Georgia. The third case challenged the constitutionality of the Texas death penalty statute. In that case, *Branch v. State*, 477 S.W.2d 932 (Tex. Crim. App. 1969), the appellant had been convicted of "rape by force" and sentenced to death. At the time of Branch's conviction, Texas was one of a few states that allowed the death penalty to be assessed for crimes other than murder.

The *Furman* case did not rule that the death penalty per se violated the Constitution. The Court, in a 5-4 decision that is famous for its lack of clarity and clear direction, ruled that the death penalty statutes violated the Eighth Amendment because they failed to provide guidance to juries who make decisions about who is sentenced to death and who is not. This lack of guidance can too easily lead to capricious and arbitrary sentences. The *Furman* decision in effect struck down all the death penalty statutes in the United States at that time because none of them had provisions to guide a jury's discretion in making the ultimate decision of who should live and who should die.

Like lawmakers in many states, the Texas legislature went to the drawing board in the wake of *Furman* and re-drafted the capital sentencing law to respond to the Supreme Court's concerns. It was not an easy task because the Court offered few suggestions as to how states could rewrite their laws to pass constitutional muster. States took essentially one of two different approaches. One type of statute provided a mandatory death penalty for certain designated capital offenses, thereby eliminating the need for juries to exercise any discretion. The other approach was to require the jury to consider specific criteria, written in the statute, during the sentencing decision. In 1976, the U.S. Supreme Court considered five death penalty cases involving new capital punishment statutes. The Court ruled that mandatory death penalty laws were unconstitutional but that guided discretion statutes were constitutional.

One of the statutes ruled constitutional in 1976 was the newly revamped section 19.03 of the Texas Penal Code in the case *Jurek v. State*, 428 U.S. 262 (1976). Section 19.03(a) restricts the class of crimes for which the death penalty can be assessed to intentionally or knowingly committing a murder in eight situations:

(1) murder of a peace officer or firefighter;
(2) murder in the course of committing or attempting to commit kidnapping, burglary, robbery, aggravated sexual assault, arson, or obstruction or retaliation;
(3) murder for remuneration;
(4) murder while escaping or attempting to escape from a penal institution;
(5) murder of an employee of a correctional institution by an inmate or murder by an inmate with the intent to establish, maintain or participate in a combination or in the profits of a combination;

(6) murder by an inmate who is already incarcerated for murder under section 19.02 or 19.03 or murder by an inmate who is serving a life sentence or a term of 99 years for an offense under sections 20.04 (aggravated kidnapping), 22.021 (aggravated sexual assault), or 29.03 (aggravated robbery);
(7) murder of more than one person when the murders are committed during the same criminal transaction or pursuant to the same scheme or course of conduct;
(8) murder of an individual under six years old.

The state legislature has amended the list of capital murders several times since the statute was originally enacted. In 1993, it added language to 19.03(a)(5) that makes it a capital murder for an inmate to kill another person with the intent to establish, participate or maintain a combination. The legislature was concerned about the number of murders committed in Texas prisons and jails by prison gang members. Subsection (6) was also added in 1993 to deal with the growing problem of prison violence. Subsection (7) was added in 1985 to include multiple murders. Subsection (8) was added in 1993 to make the murder of a child under six a capital homicide.

Article 37.071(b) of the Texas Code of Criminal Procedure completes the law of capital punishment. Under this statute, as it was originally enacted, the same jurors who convicted the defendant had to answer three questions during the punishment phase of the trial:

(1) Whether the defendant's conduct that caused the death of the deceased was committed deliberately and with the reasonable expectation that the death of the deceased or another person would result;
(2) whether there is a probability that the defendant would commit acts of violence that would constitute a continuing threat to society;
(3) if raised by the evidence, whether the conduct of the defendant in killing the deceased was unreasonable in response to the provocation, if any, of the deceased.

If the jury found unanimously beyond a reasonable doubt that the answer to all three questions is "yes," the court was required to impose the death sentence. However, if ten jurors returned a negative answer to any issue, the court was required to issue a life sentence. Jurors could not be informed about the consequences of their votes.

Unlike the other capital punishment laws that were declared constitutional in 1976, the Texas statute was not based on the Model Penal Code. In fact, the Texas death penalty law differs significantly from capital punishment laws in all the other states except Oregon. Under the Model Penal Code and in states with statutes like Georgia and Florida, which were also declared constitutional in 1976, during the punishment phase the jury hears evidence in mitigation of the offense and evidence in aggravation of the offense. A jury must find beyond a reasonable doubt that a certain number (depending on the jurisdiction) of aggravating factors exist before a death sentence can be imposed. In some statutory schemes jurors must weigh the aggravating factors against the mitigating factors. The Model Penal Code's aggravating factors track the list of eight types of capital murder found in section 19.03 of the T.P.C. The mitigating factors include such items as:

- the defendant had no significant prior criminal history;
- the murder was committed while the defendant was under the influence of extreme emotional stress or disturbance;
- the victim participated in the homicidal act or consented to it;
- the murder was committed under circumstances, which the defendant believed to provide moral justification;
- the defendant was an accomplice with another and his involvement was relatively minor;
- the defendant acted under duress or domination;
- the defendant's judgment was impaired because of a mental disease or intoxication;
- the defendant was a young person.

In *Jurek v. State*, the Supreme Court decided that the constitutionality of the Texas law turned on whether the three questions to be presented to the jury allowed it to consider mitigating factors in favor of granting the defendant a life sentence. The Court had ruled in *Woodson v. North Carolina*, 428 U.S. 280 (1976) that a death penalty statute must allow the jury to consider mitigating circumstances surrounding the crime and the offender. The Court concluded that the second question outlined in article 37.071 of the Code of Criminal Procedure concerning future dangerousness required a jury to consider mitigating factors. The U.S. Supreme Court also relied on assurances provided by the Texas Court of Criminal Appeals when it ruled on the constitutionality of the new state law in *Jurek v. State*, 522 S.W.2d 934 (Tex. Crim. App. 1975). The Court of Criminal Appeals stated in its opinion that it intended to interpret the second question about future dangerousness so as to allow a defendant to bring mitigating circumstances to a jury's attention. The Supreme Court declared the Texas statute constitutional.

Following *Jurek*, the Court of Criminal Appeals addressed several challenges that article 37.071 violated the Eighth Amendment by failing to instruct the jury sufficiently about the need to consider mitigating evidence. In each of the cases, the Texas court ruled that the Eighth Amendment does not require a separate jury instruction concerning mitigating evidence. In 1989, the U.S. Supreme Court decided *Penry v. Lynaugh*, 492 U.S. 302 (1989) which involved a Texas death sentenced inmate who had presented evidence that he was mentally retarded, suffered from organic brain damage resulting in poor impulse control, had an inability to learn from experience, and was seriously abused as a child. At the punishment phase of his trial for capital murder, the trial judge submitted the three statutory questions required by article 37.071 but refused Penry's request for an additional jury instruction about his mitigating evidence. The Supreme Court held the Texas sentencing scheme unconstitutional, as applied to Penry, because jurors were not provided a vehicle to consider his mitigation evidence. Penry's evidence went beyond the scope of the three questions, which made it difficult for the jury to consider mitigation adequately in deciding life or death.

In 1993, the Texas legislature responded to the *Penry* decision by revising article 37.071. The revision affects capital murder cases for crimes committed after September 1, 1991. An already complicated set of instructions on punishment became even more complicated. In the new scheme, under article 37.071(b) the jury is presented <u>two</u> questions to answer during punishment deliberations:

(1) whether there is a probability that the defendant would commit criminal acts of violence that would constitute a continuing threat to society; and
(2) in cases where the jury charge at the guilt or innocence stage permitted the jury to find the defendant guilty as a party under sections 7.01 and 7.02 of the Penal Code, whether the defendant actually caused the death of the deceased or did not actually cause the death of the deceased but intended to kill the deceased or another or anticipated that a human life would be taken.

Article 37.071 states that the court must charge a jury that it should consider all the evidence submitted during both the guilt/ innocence and punishments stages, including evidence of the defendant's background or character or the circumstances surrounding the crime that militates for or mitigates against the imposition of the death penalty. The jury cannot answer "yes" to the two questions unless it agrees unanimously. A "no" answer requires a vote of at least ten jurors.

Finally, and most importantly in terms of complying with the *Penry* case, if the jury answers in the affirmative to both of the two questions, it must answer a third question:

Whether, taking into consideration all of the evidence, including the circumstances of the offense, the defendant's character and background, and the personal moral culpability of the defendant, there is sufficient mitigating circumstance or circumstances to warrant that a sentence of life imprisonment rather than a death sentence be imposed.

The jury cannot answer "no" to the third question unless it agrees unanimously and may not answer "yes" unless ten or more jurors agree. The judge must sentence the offender to death if the jury responded "no" to the third issue and to life if the jury responded "yes." The Texas Court of Criminal Appeals automatically reviews a conviction and sentence to death. With the exception of Oregon, death penalty law in Texas remains very different from the other 37 states that have capital punishment and from the federal death penalty statute.

The 1999 Texas legislature amended article 37.071(e), to require a judge, upon request from defense counsel, to tell the jury that if it should decide that circumstances warrant a life sentence, the defendant will not become eligible for release on parole until the actual time he or she serves equals 40 years, without consideration of good time credits. Eligibility for parole does not guarantee that parole will be granted.

Felony-Murder Doctrine

According to the Texas capital punishment statute, murders committed during or fleeing from the commission of certain serious felonies can be punished by death. Murders committed during the commission of or fleeing from the scene of felonies not enumerated in section 19.03(a)(2) can be punished as first-degree felonies. From a defendant's perspective, it becomes very important to clearly define the scope of the felony murder doctrine, especially for those defendants who face a death sentence. Since many felony murders in Texas can be categorized as capital crimes, the cases that have contributed to developing the felony murder doctrine generally concern defendants who are fighting for their lives.

In order for a murder to be committed during the course of a robbery, under section 19.03(a)(2), the murder must have occurred during a theft involving the use of force or threats of serious bodily injury. The intent to rob the victim must have been formed before or concurrent with the murder. The robbery itself need not have occurred before the murder. It may have occurred during the murder or in immediate flight from the murder. The prosecution's job is to convince the jury beyond a reasonable doubt that the defendant intended to rob the victim before or during the time he killed the victim. The same is true for other capital felony murders: the intent to kidnap, commit burglary, sexually assault, rob, commit arson, obstruction, or retaliation must have been formed before or at the time of the murder. The actus reus of the felony underlying the capital murder charge did not have to occur before or during the victim's murder. Sometimes the jury has a difficult decision to make.

In *Santellan v. State*, 939 S.W.2d 156 (Tex. Crim. App. 1997), the defendant argued that he was not guilty of capital murder because there was insufficient evidence that he intended to kidnap his victim/girlfriend before he murdered her. Santellan went to his girlfriend's place of employment to say goodbye. He ended up shooting her. Unclear in his mind as to whether she was alive or dead, he put her in his car, and drove her to a motel where he sexually abused her corpse. He maintained that he intended to kill her but had not intended to kidnap her. The difference for Santellan was a first-degree felony punishable by 5 to 99 years in prison or a capital murder verdict punishable by death. The Court of Criminal Appeals upheld the capital murder conviction.

Alvarado, who was seventeen at the time of his offense, argued that he had not intended to rob his victims before he killed them. The jury rejected his claims and sentenced him to death. The Court of Appeals upheld the verdict in *Alvarado v. State*, 912 S.W.2d 199 (Tex. Crim. App. 1995). The evidence showed that Alvarado and his accomplices felt cheated by the victims from whom they had purchased drugs. The armed themselves with knives and went to the victims' home with the intent of killing them. Immediately after the murders, they searched the house and stole items from the victims. The Court concluded there was sufficient evidence for a jury to find that Alvarado formed the intent to rob either before or during the murders.

In *Gonzales v. State*, 905 S.W.2d 4 (Tex. Crim. App. 1995), Gonzales went to the home of his victims with the intent to kill them. The victims' daughter admitted him into the home while the victims were asleep. She aided and encouraged the killing of her parents. Gonzales was convicted of killing his victims during the commission of a burglary because the court ruled the daughter did not have the authority to consent to Gonzales entering the home. The daughter's participation in the crime rendered her consent to entry ineffective. The underlying offense was burglary of a habitation under section 30.02: a person commits a burglary if he enters a habitation without the effective consent of the owner with the intent to commit a felony or theft.

The impact of the felony murder doctrine is far reaching. The more "liberally" the courts interpret it, the wider the net of the death penalty statute. District attorneys decide how aggressively to pursue the doctrine in their counties. Many offenders on death row have been convicted of felony murders, making the doctrine an important legal issue in many capital felony prosecutions.

Other Capital Murder Issues

Section 19.03(a)(7)(A) provides that a person commits capital murder if he intentionally or knowingly murders more than one person during the same criminal transaction or during different criminal transactions but the murders are committed pursuant to the same scheme or course of conduct. The legislature did not define the term "same criminal transaction." Billie Coble argued that the term requires a continuity of time and place. He was convicted of capital murder in *Coble v. State*, 871 S.W.2d 192 (Tex. Crim. App. 1993), after murdering his ex-wife, her brother and her parents over a span of three hours. The murders were committed in different locations but in the same neighborhood. The Court of Appeals concluded that the jury had sufficient evidence to find the murders occurred as part of the same criminal transaction because they were committed in close proximity to each other, within a few hours of each other and constituted a continuous and uninterrupted series of events.

The appellant in *Corwin v. State*, 870 S.W.2d 23 (Tex. Crim. App. 1993) was also convicted of murdering more than one person pursuant to the same course of conduct or scheme. He had abducted, sexually assaulted, and killed two women over the course of nine months. During those nine months, he had also attempted to abduct a third woman, and when he could not, he killed her. Corwin claimed that the term "same scheme or course of conduct" was so indefinite he could not tell whether his conduct in killing more than one person during different criminal transactions was a capital offense. The Texas Court of Criminal Appeals reviewed the legislative history of the penal provision and concluded in its opinion that the legislature intended to target serial murders. The Court agreed there may be some difficult fact situations as time and distance between murders increases, but in Corwin's case, the court found the jury had sufficient evidence that he killed as part of the same scheme or course of conduct.

McCollister was convicted of capital murder for killing his 23-month-old stepdaughter. He argued in *McCollister v. State*, 933 S.W.2d 170 (Tex. App. - Eastland 1996), that the indictment failed to allege he had knowledge that his murder victim was under the age of six years old. The appellate court ruled that the plain language of section 19.03(a)(8) does not require the accused must have known the victim was under six to be guilty of capital murder. Knowledge of the victim's age is not an element of the offense.

In *Underwood v. State*, 853 S.W.2d 858 (Tex. App. - Fort Worth 1993), the court defined "remuneration" in section 19.03(a)(3) to include more than pecuniary gain. In that prosecution for solicitation of murder, the defendant offered to kill someone for the offeree if the offeree would kill someone for the defendant. "Remuneration" includes any benefit or compensation received because of the killing. A wife can be found guilty of murder for remuneration for killing her husband for the proceeds of his life insurance benefits. An actor's unilateral conduct in killing for gain or benefit can lead to a capital murder charge under 19.03(a)(3). *Beets v. State*, 767 S.W.2d 711 (Tex. Crim. App. 1987).

An important aspect of Texas death penalty law is the law of parties and which applies to capital murder. In order to impose culpability on a defendant as a party to the crime of capital murder, the State must prove that one party committed the murder, and that the defendant, with the intent to promote or assist the murder, aided, encouraged, or solicited the other party. The evidence must show that at the time of the crime, the parties were acting together, each doing some part of the execution of their common purpose. Persons convicted under the law of parties can also be sentenced to death.

David Cameron was convicted of capital murder for his participation in the robbery and murder of two victims. The evidence showed that Cameron agreed with his friends to rob the victims, brought knives to the scene of the crime, at one point wrestled with one of the murder victims, and robbed the victims after the murders were completed. The evidence did not show Cameron had actually committed the murders. The court concluded there was sufficient evidence that Cameron intended to facilitate the murders. His conviction for capital murder was upheld in *Cameron v. State*, 925 S.W.2d 246 (Tex. App. – El Paso 1995).

FINAL COMMENTS ON THE MURDER STATUTES

Before wading into the death penalty debate, it is important to understand the law of murder and capital murder. What distinguishes a first-degree felony murder in Texas from a capital murder? How does jurors go about punishing an offender who they have just convicted of capital murder? The process by which a person is sentenced to death or life is an important component in the debate. No process is full proof. How a jury answers the special questions during the punishment phase will depend on the composition of that 12-member body, how they interact, communicate, and compromise. It is a tremendously complex exchange, and a human being's life is in the balance.

The Texas death penalty has generated a lot of court opinions and has been the object of both criticism and support throughout the country. The mechanics of how a defendant is convicted of a capital crime and sentenced are central to the issue. We can question whether the state should have the power to take away a person's life. For those who decide there are circumstances that warrant a death sentence, the issue becomes whether the process by which someone is sentenced to death is as fair as it should be, and, if it is not, how can it be made better. How fair must the process be? Are there components of the process that will remain problematic no matter what we do to improve them?

MULTIPLE CHOICE QUESTIONS

1. In Texas, the capital murder statute states that the State must prove at least one aggravating factor and disprove any mitigating factors in order to establish a capital murder.

    a. True
    b. False

2. The capital punishment law in Texas is similar to capital punishment statutes in other states.

    a. True
    b. False

3. Hector was discharged from prison and flagged down a cabdriver who agreed to take him from Huntsville to Dallas. Hector realized that he would not be able to pay the full fair. When the cab arrived in Dallas, Hector decided to assault the cabdriver. He did not want to kill the cabby, just do enough harm to get away quickly without paying the fair. Unfortunately for Hector, the cabby was a hemophiliac. Hector's blow to his head left him to bleed to death. Hector is guilty of:

   a. murder, he never intended to kill the cabby, only rob him and put him temporarily out of commission.
   b. capital murder because he killed the cabby during a robbery.
   c. capital murder because he attacked a man with serious health problems, making the murder particularly heinous.
   d. manslaughter because he recklessly created a risk but never intended a murder.

4. Jerry was out late at night driving drunk, again. He has had several DWI convictions. He pulled into the McDonald's parking lot and went inside to order a Big Mac. He forgot to put his emergency break on and the car rolled down a noticeable incline onto the street. It plowed into another car, killing the driver. Jerry is guilty of:

   a. criminally negligent homicide.
   b. manslaughter.
   c. murder.
   d. vehicular homicide.

5. Wally decided that the members of his prison gang needed better discipline. He "requested" Rocky Hardnose to "rub out" a dissident gang member. Rocky dutifully complied. Wally is guilty of:

   a. no crime, he did not commit the murder.
   b. murder.
   c. capital murder.
   d. manslaughter.

6. A Texas jury is not advised when they begin deliberations on punishment in a capital murder trial about the consequences of the questions they must answer under the Code of Criminal Procedure.

   a. True
   b. False

7. The 1976 Texas capital punishment case that was reviewed by the U.S. Supreme Court when the Court decided the Texas statute passed constitutional muster was:

   a. *Gregg v. Texas.*
   b. *Jurek v. Texas.*
   c. *Proffitt v. Texas.*
   d. *Furman v. Texas.*

8. The crime of voluntary manslaughter has been totally eliminated in Texas.

    a. True, there are no provisions recognizing murders committed with adequate provocation and in the heat of passion.
    b. True, all murders are equal.
    c. False, voluntary manslaughter is no longer a separate crime but evidence of the elements of voluntary manslaughter can be introduced during the punishment phase of a murder trial in mitigation of punishment.
    d. False, manslaughter has now been redefined to include both voluntary and involuntary manslaughter.

9. Prosecutors are required under the law in Texas to ask for the death penalty in every capital murder case.

    a. True
    b. False

10. Louise decided to knock-off her wealthy husband in hopes of inheriting his fortunes while she was still young and healthy. She decided to commit the murder herself and not hire a hit man. She successfully murdered her husband. Louise is guilty of:

    a. capital murder for remuneration.
    b. murder because the money was adequate provocation.
    c. capital murder as a felony-murder, she murdered intending to steal his money.
    d. murder because she intentionally killed her husband.

CHAPTER TEN

CRIMES AGAINST PERSONS: CRIMINAL SEXUAL CONDUCT AND OTHERS

INTRODUCTION

This chapter looks at the crimes of assault and sexual assault. After homicide, assault crimes are considered the most dangerous offenses. Sexual assault, in particular, is a difficult crime to prosecute. It is a complicated criminal statute that is supplemented by various articles from the Texas Code of Criminal Procedure. The crime of assault in Texas consolidates the common law crimes of assault and battery into one statute. Both sexual assault and assault can be aggravated into more serious offenses if certain specific statutory elements were present at the time the crimes were committed.

SEXUAL ASSAULT

The History

Penal Code sections 22.011 and 22.021 govern the offenses of sexual assault and aggravated sexual assault. They are among the most complex statutes in the code, in part because the state legislature has amended them so frequently. When it comes to reviewing the cases that have interpreted these two statutes, it is sometimes difficult to know which court opinions construe which statute.

The amendments to the sexual assault statutes reflect how society's awareness and perspective have changed. When the Texas Penal Code was totally revamped in 1974, the statutes were labeled rape and aggravated rape. At that time, rape was defined as intercourse with a woman other than the defendant's spouse without her consent. The statute required proof that the force used against the victim overcame what earnest resistance might reasonably be expected under the circumstances. Rape of a child was defined as intercourse with a female child who was not the defendant's wife and was under the age of 17. Lack of consent was not an element of the crime because children were deemed unable to consent. Aggravated rape was defined as rape or rape of a child plus certain aggravating factors. In 1974, the Texas legislature created the separate crimes of sexual abuse and aggravated sexual abuse. Sexual abuse was essentially defined as deviate sexual intercourse with any non-consenting partner. Deviate sexual intercourse included acts of sodomy.

As they interpreted the 1974 rape and sexual abuse statutes, Texas courts focused primarily on the nature and strength of the force or threats used to compel a victim to submit. In *Rucker v. State*, 599 S.W.2d 581 (Tex. Crim. App. 1979), the Texas Court of Criminal Appeals ruled that a victim who was badly beaten by her attacker <u>after</u> he raped her did not suffer an aggravated rape because there was no evidence that a threat of serious bodily injury or harm was used to compel her to submit. The court decided that the aggravating element of threatening death, serious bodily injury, or kidnapping could be satisfied only if it was used to compel the victim to submit to the act. That decision was highly controversial and was followed by significant legislative amendments to the statutes in both 1981 and 1983.

In 1981, the rape statutes were amended to permit conviction if the defendant compelled the victim to submit by any threat, communicated by actions, words, or deeds, that would prevent resistance by a woman of ordinary resolution, under the same or similar circumstances, because of a reasonable fear of harm. Language was eliminated that the force must have been sufficient to overcome such earnest resistance as might reasonably be expected. The aggravated rape statute, which already permitted conviction for serious bodily harm, was amended to permit conviction because of acts, words, or deeds that placed the victim in fear that death, serious bodily injury or kidnapping would be inflicted upon <u>anyone</u> if she did not submit. These amendments allowed juries and judges to consider not only the injuries and express verbal threats that victims suffered but also the defendant's overall conduct as manifested by his acts, words, and deeds. Prior to 1981, the defendant's violence had to compel the victim's submission. After 1981, if a rape occurred and there was violence, the crime was aggravated rape, regardless of whether the violence was used to compel submission or for some other reason. The 1981 amendments added an additional factor that could aggravate rape - the use or exhibition of a deadly weapon during the crime.

The 1983 legislature continued to pass significant amendments. It combined rape and sexual abuse into one statute and changed its title to sexual assault. Aggravated rape and sexual abuse were combined into one aggravated sexual assault statute. The legislature amended the provisions that addressed threats used to compel submission to include threats of force that a victim believed the defendant had the present ability to execute. This change went further than the 1981 amendment that required a threat to meet the level that would prevent resistance by a woman of ordinary resolution. The 1983 statute replaced the objective standard of a person of ordinary resolution with the victim's subjective belief in the attacker's ability to execute the threat. The amendments also created a gender-neutral statute. Both men and women can commit sexual assault, and both men and women can be victims of sexual assault.

Recognizing that nonconsensual sexual activity is inherently violent, the 1981 and 1983 changes refocused the crime of sexual assault away from an emphasis on how much force was used against the victim to the nonconsensual nature of the offense. The statute evolved quickly as society learned more about the nature of sexual violence. In 1991, the Texas statute was amended to eliminate the marital exemption provision, so spouses can be convicted of sexually assaulting their mates.

> **Exercise:**
> Read Article 21.31 of the Code of Criminal Procedure. It was added in 1987 and requires persons indicted under sections 21.11, 22.011, or 22.021 of the Penal Code to undergo a medical test for sexually transmitted diseases.

The Sexual Assault Statute

Section 22.011 defines sexual assault in Texas. A person commits the offense if that person, without the victim's consent:

(1) intentionally or knowingly
(A) causes the penetration of the anus or female sexual organ of a victim by any means;
(B) causes the penetration of the mouth of a victim by the sexual organs of the actor;
(C) causes the sexual organ of a victim to contact or penetrate the mouth, anus, or sexual organ of another person, including the actor; or
(2) intentionally or knowingly
(A) causes the penetration of the anus or female sexual organ of a child by any means;
(B) causes the penetration of the mouth of a child by the sexual organ of the actor;
(C) causes the sexual organ of a child to contact or penetrate the mouth, anus, or sexual organ of another person, including the actor;
(D) causes the anus of a child to contact the mouth, anus, or sexual organ of another person, including the actor;
(E) causes the mouth of a child to contact the anus or sexual organ of another person, including the actor.

"Without the consent of the other person" is defined to include ten specific circumstances:

(1) the use of physical force or violence;
(2) threatening to use force or violence and the victim believes the actor has the present ability to execute the threat;
(3) the actor knows the victim is unconscious or physically unable to resist;
(4) the actor knows the victim suffers from a mental disease and is not capable of appraising the nature of the act or of resisting it;
(5) the actor knows the victim is unaware that the sexual assault is occurring;
(6) the actor has impaired the victim by administering a substance without the victim's knowledge;
(7) threatening to use force or violence against any person and the victim believes the actor has the present ability to execute the threat;
(8) the actor is a public servant who coerces the victim to submit or participate;
(9) the actor is a mental health service provider who exploits a patient's or former patient's emotional dependency;
(10) the actor is a clergyman who exploits the victim's emotional dependency in the clergyman's role as spiritual advisor.

The mens rea for the crime of sexual assault is intentionally or knowingly. The State does not have to prove that the defendant both intentionally and knowingly had intercourse and intentionally and knowingly compelled the victim to submit.

Lack of Consent

Lack of consent is determined by the ten statutory conditions, one of which must be proved beyond a reasonable doubt before there can be a conviction. If force or violence was used to compel submission, the State does not need to prove or allege the defendant used any specific level of force or physical violence. The State only has to show that the defendant used force or violence that was directed at the victim.

If lack of consent is based on evidence that the actor knew the victim was physically unable to resist, there is no requirement that the actor used or threatened force, nor that the victim resisted. To show that a victim was physically unable to resist, the State only needs to prove that the actor knew the victim was physically impaired and was not able to reasonably resist.

Suarez v. State, 901 S.W.2d 712 (Tex. App. - Corpus Christi 1995), involved charges of sexual assault against a midwife who assaulted his patient during a pelvic examination. The evidence showed that during the examination, while the patient was on the table and her heels in the stirrups, Suarez used his fingers to inappropriately touch her female sexual organs while telling the patient that he was conducting a thorough exam. The patient was pregnant and feared that Suarez might harm her baby if she moved or protested. The patient did not tell Suarez to stop because she was frozen with fear. In her testimony, she asserted that she did not consent to his actions. An exam that should have taken less than a minute took about 30 minutes. A nurse was not in the room, and the door was closed. Suarez argued there was no evidence that the victim was physically unable to resist. She was not tied to the table. He made no threats and used no violence. He had no weapon. The appellate court affirmed his conviction because it found there was sufficient evidence that the victim was physically unable to resist. She was pregnant on an examination table with her legs in stirrups, which made it difficult for her to sit up with Suarez standing over her, and she was concerned about the safety of her unborn baby.

If the defendant knew the victim suffered from a mental disease or defect and was unable to appraise the situation or resist, the act is also considered nonconsensual if the State proves that the defendant knew the victim was unable to resist or understand the nature of what was happening. The statute does not treat mentally retarded victims like children. In *Garcia v. State*, 661 S.W.2d 96 (Tex. Crim. App. 1983), Garcia's conviction was reversed by the Court of Criminal Appeals because there was insufficient evidence the defendant knew the victim was mentally retarded and unable to appraise the act of sexual intercourse or resist it.

Child Victims

In cases of child victims, there is no need to prove lack of consent because victims are unable to consent according to law. A child is defined as a person under 17 years old who is not the spouse of the actor. It is not necessary that the defendant knew the child was under 17. There is no mistake of fact defense in Texas, according to *Jackson v. State*, 889 S.W.2d 615 (Tex. App. - Houston [14th Dist.] 1994).

There are two defenses to a charge of sexual assault against a child. A crime was not committed if the contact between the child and the adult consisted of medical care for the child and did not include any contact between the child's anus or sexual organ and the mouth, anus, or sexual organ of the health care provider. This defense was unnecessary under the 1974 version of the law because that statute required that the actor intend to arouse or gratify the victim sexually. Again, it is apparent how the law has changed to reflect society's more sophisticated understanding of what constitutes a sexual assault. No longer does the mens rea require a showing that the defendant intended to arouse or gratify the victim.

The other defense is if the defendant was not more than three years older than the victim and the victim was a child of 14 years of age or older at the time of the act. This is an affirmative defense that the defendant must prove by a preponderance of the evidence. The age difference was originally only two years but was extended to three in 1993. The defense is only available to a defendant if he or she was not required at the time of the offense to register for life as a sex offender and was not a person who had a reportable conviction or adjudication for an offense under the sexual assault statute.

A third defense to a charge of sexual assault against a child is no longer available because the Texas legislature repealed the provision in 1993. Prior to 1993, a defendant could introduce evidence of a child victim's promiscuity, as long as the victim was over 14 years old and the acts of promiscuity occurred prior to the charge against the defendant. Texas courts had interpreted the defense to require more than a few prior sexual experiences. The term was defined to mean a variety of sexual behaviors over a reasonable period of time with a variety of partners. The promiscuity defense proved troublesome for the courts. Critics of the provision argued it was out of step with the direction Texas law had been heading and behind legal developments in the rest of the country where the defense was generally out of favor. The defense was repealed by the same legislature that raised the age difference defense to three years.

The Aggravated Sexual Assault Statute

Section 22.021 defines the crime of aggravated sexual assault. It begins by incorporating all of the requirements of sexual assault and adding certain specified aggravating factors. Any one of these factors can aggravate an assault, and it can occur at any point during the assault. It does not have to compel submission to the attack. If an aggravating factor occurs at the beginning of the assault but does not continue throughout, the offense is still considered an aggravated crime. In *McAfee v. State*, 624 S.W.2d 776 (Tex. App. - Houston [14th Dist.] 1981), the appellant argued that he should not be convicted of aggravated rape because his threats to kill the victim were made 30 to 45 minutes before he actually raped her. The appellate court rejected his argument, finding that his threats and actions were all a part of an episode that culminated in an aggravated rape.

A sexual assault becomes aggravated if the actor:

(1) causes serious bodily injury or attempts to cause the death of the victim or another person during the same criminal episode;
(2) by acts or words places the victim in fear that death, serious bodily injury, or kidnapping will be imminently inflicted on any person;
(3) by acts or words occurring in the victim's presence, threatens to cause the death, serious bodily injury, or kidnapping of any person;

(4) uses or exhibits a deadly weapon in the course of the assault;
(5) acts in concert with another person to sexually assault the victim during the course of the same criminal episode (gang-type rapes).

A sexual assault is also aggravated if the victim was under the age of 14 or 65 years of age or older. In 1999, the legislature amended the statute to provide that a sexual assault is aggravated if the defendant administered or provided rohypnol or gamma hydroxybutrate (GHB) to the victim with the intent of facilitating the crime of sexual assault.

Acts or words that threaten do not have to be express or verbal. Threats can be inferred from the totality of the circumstances, including the defendant's words, acts, and deeds. The issue is whether given all that transpired, was the victim placed in fear of imminent serious bodily injury, death, or kidnapping. In *Seek v. State,* 646 S.W.2d 557 (Tex. App. - Houston [1st] 1982), Seek argued he was not guilty of aggravated rape because he did not use a weapon or suggest that he had one, nor did he compel submission by an express verbal threat. The evidence showed that Seek threw the victim to the floor, hit her in the face and choked her with his hands. The victim testified she feared for her safety. The court concluded that by his acts, words, or deeds, the appellant put the victim in fear for her life, committing the crime of aggravated rape. A jury could infer from the totality of circumstances that Seek's acts and deeds placed the victim in fear.

Another aggravating factor involves threats of future death, serious injury, or kidnapping to any person. There is no requirement that the threats be of imminent harm; however, the threats must be made in the victim's presence.

The 1999 Texas legislature created a new offense, section 38.17, that punishes persons who fail to stop or report the aggravated sexual abuse of a child if they could have done so without placing themselves in danger of serious injury or death. The offense is not restricted to persons who have a legal or statutory duty to act or have assumed care, custody, or control of the child. The crime is punished as a Class A misdemeanor.

Important Evidentiary Issues

The Outcry Statement

Because the only witnesses to sexual assault crimes are often the victim and the offender, the law is concerned about the need to substantiate or corroborate a lone victim's allegations. Article 38.07 of the Texas Code of Criminal Procedure provides that a conviction under sections 22.011 or 22.021 can be supported on the uncorroborated testimony of the victim if the victim informed any person, other than the defendant, of the offense within one year after the date on which the offense occurred. That requirement is waived if the victim was younger than 18 years old at the time of the sexual assault. This evidentiary requirement is called the outcry statement. The one-year reporting period went into effect in 1993 and expanded what was previously a six-month reporting period. Also, in 1993, the legislature raised the maximum age for which no corroboration is required from 14 to 18 years old.

If the victim made a report within a year of the offense, there is no need for corroborating evidence. If a report was not made, article 38.07 requires some kind of corroboration. Without it, there can be no conviction. Corroborating evidence only needs to connect the defendant to the offense. In *Nemecek v. State*, 621 S.W.2d 404 (Tex. Crim. App. 1980), the appellant admitted to having sexual intercourse with the 13 year old child victim but alleged that it was with the child's consent. The child did not make an outcry statement within the time period specified in article 38.07 so that corroborating evidence was necessary to support Nemecek's conviction. The court concluded that Nemecek's own admissions were sufficient corroboration of the victim's testimony.

If there was a lapse of time between the sexual assault and the victim's report, article 38.07 requires that the jury be instructed it may consider the lapse in evaluating the victim's credibility. Article 38.072 of the Code of Criminal Procedure addresses a child victim's hearsay statements. If a child victim described the offense to a person over 18 years old other than the defendant, those statements are admissible even though they are hearsay, if the child was under the age of 12.

Article 38.071 of the Texas Code of Criminal Procedure protects children who are victims of sexual assault. Under certain circumstances, it allows a videotape of a child's statement to be introduced into evidence in lieu of the child testifying in court. It also allows a child to be questioned by closed circuit television as opposed to appearing live in the courtroom.

Victim's Past Conduct

Another very important evidentiary matter in sexual assault cases concerns the admissibility of evidence about the victim's prior sexual conduct. Rule 412 of the Texas Rules of Criminal Evidence governs the admissibility of such evidence. It provides that reputation or opinion evidence about the victim's past sexual behavior is inadmissible. Evidence of specific instances of a victim's prior sexual behavior is also inadmissible except under certain narrow circumstances, and only if the court first determines that the probative value of that evidence outweighs any danger of unfair prejudice to the victim.

To be admissible under one of the two narrow exceptions, evidence of specific past instances might be necessary to rebut or explain scientific or medical evidence offered by the State. For instance, if the State introduces evidence concerning tears and lacerations to the victim's vagina on the theory that they were caused by the defendant, the defendant could introduce evidence of an alternative cause of the injuries. Prior sexual conduct is also admissible if the conduct was with the accused and the accused raises consent as a defense. The evidence is admissible only if it exposes the victim's bias or a motive to testify falsely. Decisions about the admissibility of evidence about a victim's prior sexual conduct are made outside the presence of the jury in a hearing before the judge, closed to the public. The record of that hearing is sealed from public view and is only for review by the appellate court, if necessary. The rule is strictly enforced. Rule 412 minimizes the embarrassment and humiliation suffered by sexual assault victims and seeks to encourage victims to report sexual assaults to authorities.

> **Exercises:**
> Read article 38.071 in the Code of Criminal Procedure and outline the circumstance in which videotapes and testimony by closed circuit television can be used in cases involving child victims of sexual assault crimes. Read the U.S. Supreme Court's decision *Maryland v. Craig*, 497 U.S. 836, 110 S.Ct. 3157, 111 L.Ed.2d 666 (1990) to understand the reason why article 38.071 provides so many safeguards for both the child victim and the defendant.
>
> Read two other important Penal Code provisions dealing with sexual misconduct: section 21.11 Indecency with a Child and section 25.02 Prohibited Sexual Conduct. Notice how those statutes address slightly different but related types of behavior from sections 22.011 and 22.021.

Sex Offender Registration

State legislatures throughout the country have examined sexual assault statutes in recent years to find ways to better protect communities. The U.S. Congress passed legislation in 1994, 1995, and 1996 that requires states to create registries of certain sex offenders and establish community notification programs. As of 1996, all fifty states require sex offenders to register with local law enforcement agencies when they are on community supervision.

The Texas Sex Offender Registration Program, found in Chapter 62 of the Texas Code of Criminal Procedure, was originally enacted in 1991 and has been amended in each succeeding legislative session. In 1997, the registration requirements were made retroactive to convictions or adjudications that occurred on or after September 1, 1970. It is a multi-agency program that is administered by the Texas Department of Public Safety.

There are ten categories of sex crimes that carry a requirement to register. Convictions, adjudications, deferred adjudications, or adjudications of delinquent conduct for any offense in these categories, including attempt, conspiracy or solicitation result in registration. Offenders who commit sex crimes that are listed as sexually violent must register for the remainder of their lives. Other sex offenders must continue to register for ten years after their release or discharge from supervision or incarceration, whichever comes first.

The categories of sex crimes are:

- Indecency with a Child – Compelling Prostitution;
- Sexual Assault – Aggravated Sexual Assault;
- Prohibited Sexual Conduct – Sexual Performance by a Child;
- Aggravated Kidnapping with Intent to Violate or Abuse the Victim Sexually;
- Burglary of a Habitation with Intent to Commit a Felony Sexual Offense;
- A second conviction for Indecent Exposure;
- Unlawful Restraint, Kidnapping, or Aggravated Kidnapping if the judgment contains a finding that the victim was a child under 17;
- Any substantially similar offense committed under the laws of another jurisdiction;
- Any offense that results in a condition of parole, release on mandatory supervision, or community supervision requiring registration as a sex offender.

The violent sex crimes requiring lifetime registration are:

- Indecency with a Child by Contact;
- Compelling Prostitution of a Minor;
- Sexual Assault and Aggravated Sexual Assault, regardless of the victim's age;
- Prohibited Sexual Conduct;
- Sexual Performance by a Child;
- Possession or Promotion of Child Pornography;
- Aggravated Kidnapping with Intent to Violate or Abuse the Victim Sexually;
- Burglary of a Habitation with Intent to Commit a Felony Sexual Offense.

Sex offenders who fall within the requirements must register their address with the appropriate local law enforcement agency. They must notify authorities about any change of address. Offenders must verify their registration with local law enforcement annually, on their birthday. If the offender has two or more violent sex offender convictions, they must verify their registration every ninety days. Offenders who fail to comply with any of the registration requirements face punishment ranging from a state jail felony for those who are not required to register for a lifetime to a third-degree felony for those who must register annually for life. Offenders who must register every ninety days face a second-degree felony.

Local law enforcement agencies send registration information to the Department of Public Safety who up-date the state registry. All sex offender registration information is considered public and must be released by local law enforcement agencies upon written request, including information on adult and juvenile offenders. The public information includes the offender's name, address, offense, and his or her photograph. Information about offenders whose victims were under age 17, and whose case was dispositioned on or after September 1, 1995, is subject to publication in newspapers or on a website. Public and private schools are provided information about all offenders who live in the school district and whose victims were under age 17.

ASSAULT

Texas law does not separate the common law crimes of assault and battery into different statutes. There are two primary assault statutes: section 22.01 and 22.02. The crime of assault is defined in section 22.01 of the Penal Code and includes behavior that could be categorized as battery. Assault is committed if a person:

(1) intentionally, knowingly, or recklessly causes bodily injury to another, including the person's spouse;
(2) intentionally or knowingly threatens another with imminent bodily injury, including the person's spouse;
(3) intentionally or knowingly causes physical contact with another when the person knows or should reasonably believe that the other will regard the contact as offensive or provocative.

The mens rea requirement for causing bodily injury is intentionally, knowingly, or recklessly. The mens rea requirement for threatening to cause injury or causing offensive or provocative contact is intentionally or knowingly. A person cannot recklessly threaten or cause offensive contact.

An offense under subsection (1) is a Class A misdemeanor. It is a third-degree felony if it was committed against a public servant while the servant was discharging his official duties or in retaliation for an action taken by a public servant in the performance of his official duties. It is also a third-degree felony if it was committed against a family member and the defendant had previously been convicted of an offense against a family member.

Section 22.02 provides that a person commits aggravated assault if the person:

(1) causes serious bodily injury to another, including the person's spouse; or
(2) uses or exhibits a deadly weapon during the commission of the assault.

A conviction under section 22.02 is a second-degree felony unless it was committed against a public servant while he performing official duties or in retaliation for performing those duties, which would make it a first-degree felony. It is also a first-degree felony if it was committed in retaliation against or on account of service as a witness, prospective witness, informant, or against a person who reported a crime to the authorities.

Deadly Weapon

What can be considered a deadly weapon is important in an aggravated assault charge. In *Powell v. State*, 939 S.W.2d 713 (Tex. App. - El Paso 1997), the appellant was convicted of aggravated assault after repeatedly kicking a police officer with his foot. The Penal Code defines a deadly weapon in section 1.07 as anything that in the manner of use or intended use is capable of causing death or serious bodily injury. A foot is not usually considered a deadly weapon, but the court concluded that it might become a deadly weapon if used in such a way that it could cause death or serious injuries. The evidence showed that Powell's foot caused serious injuries. A medical expert testified that Powell's blows to the victim's head with his foot were serious and could have killed the officer. The aggravated assault conviction was affirmed.

In *Gibbs v. State*, 932 S.W.2d 256 (Tex. App. - Texarkana 1996), the appellate court affirmed Gibb's aggravated assault conviction for using his truck as a deadly weapon. The evidence showed that Gibbs used his truck to back into several victims and ran forward over another victim.

The Court of Appeals upheld the aggravated assault conviction of Isaac Melonson in *Melonson v. State*, 942 S.W.2d 777 (Tex. App. - Beaumont 1997). Melonson argued that he did not participate in the use of a deadly weapon against the victim who had been beaten with a baseball bat. Melonson admitted hitting the victim and being present during the baseball bat beating but argued he was only guilty of assault. The court relied on the law of parties to affirm his conviction because he was aware that his crime partners were using a baseball bat against the victim and did not attempt to stop the attack. He had also agreed to attack the victim in order to steal his truck. The court concluded that Gibbs was acting with the other attackers, and encouraged and participated in the aggravated assault even though he did not use the bat himself.

Other Assault Statutes

If a person recklessly puts another person in imminent danger of serious bodily injury, he or she can be charged with Deadly Conduct under section 22.05. Deadly conduct also includes knowingly discharging a firearm at or in the direction of other people or a habitation, building, or vehicle and being reckless as to whether those structures are occupied. Recklessness and danger are presumed if the defendant knowingly pointed a firearm in the direction of another person whether or not the defendant believed the firearm was loaded.

Another important assault statute is section 22.04 Injury to a Child, Elderly Individual, or Disabled Individual. The statute makes it a crime to intentionally, knowingly, recklessly, or with criminal negligence cause bodily injury, serious bodily injury, or serious mental deficiency, impairment, or injury to a child, an elderly person, or a disabled person. The actus reus includes acts of omission if the defendant had a legal or statutory duty to act or assumed care for the injured person. A child is a person 14 years old or under. An elderly individual is 65 years or older. A disabled individual is a person who because of age or physical or mental disease, defect, or injury is unable to protect himself or to provide food, shelter, or medical care for himself.

What constitutes assuming care for a child was the issue in *Hawkins v. State*, 910 S.W.2d 176 (Tex. App. - Fort Worth 1995). In that case Hawkins was convicted of injury to a child by omission. Hawkins lived with Teresa Hutchins and her two children. They were not married, but he claimed the children as his own, and Hutchins used his last name. Hawkins observed several acts of abuse inflicted by Hutchins on her seven-week old son. After one such incident, Hawkins called for an ambulance and signed the medical consent form authorizing treatment for the boy. The child suffered severe brain damage, and Hutchins pled guilty to criminal charges.

Hawkins' first conviction for injury to a child was reversed by the Fort Worth Court of Appeals because it ruled that Hawkins did not have a duty to remove the child from the presence of Hutchins under the Texas Family Code. The Court of Criminal Appeals reversed the appellate court and ruled that because Hawkins was prosecuted under section 22.04 of the Penal Code, the State did not have to prove that Hawkins had a duty to care for the child under the Family Code. Hawkins went to trial again and was convicted. He filed another appeal, arguing that there was not enough evidence that he had assumed care, custody, and control of the child under section 22.04. The appellate court overruled his argument and affirmed his conviction.

Section 22.015 was added to the Penal Code in 1999. The statute makes it a separate crime to threaten a child or cause a child injury with the intent to coerce, induce, or solicit a child to actively participate in street gang activities. Threatening injury results in a state jail felony. Causing injury results in a third-degree felony. Also added to the assault statutes in 1999 was section 22.11, which makes it a third-degree felony for persons who are incarcerated in secure correctional facilities or in the Texas Youth Commission to cause another person to contact blood, semen, urine, or feces with the intent to harass, alarm, or annoy them. This statute is aimed at a significant problem in correctional institutions: prisoners who throw blood, urine, and feces at correctional officers.

> **Exercises:**
> Read section 22.07 of the Penal Code, Terroristic Threats. It covers threats to property as well as to persons. It also addresses threats that interrupt the occupation of a building, place of employment, aircraft, etc.
>
> Before section 22.015 concerning soliciting a child into gang activities was on the books, under what statutes would a D.A. prosecute a person who engaged in this behavior? What would have been the potential punishment? Assume that the child was not seriously injured.
>
> Notice several other "assault" statutes in Chapter 22 of the Penal Code: Abandoning or Endangering a Child (section 22.041); Aiding Suicide (section 22.08); Tampering with a Consumer Product (section 22.09); and Leaving a Child in a Vehicle (section 22.10).

FINAL COMMENTS ON SEXUAL ASSAULT AND ASSAULT

Sexual assault statutes have undergone tremendous reform during the last two decades. The law is a living presence. It is shaped by what we think is inappropriate behavior. It evolves as we evolve. The study of criminal law is much more than the study of statutes and legal analysis. It is the study of how society changes to meet new challenges, and how the sensibilities of human beings develop over time. Sexual assault laws are a good example of how what happens in the legislature and in the courtroom reflects what is happening in the hearts and minds of ordinary men and women.

MULTIPLE CHOICE QUESTIONS

1. To convict a person of the crime of sexual assault in Texas, there must be evidence that:

    a. the victim resisted the attacker to the utmost.
    b. the accused used physical force against the victim.
    c. the accused made threats of force and the victim believed the accused had the present ability to execute the threats.
    d. either b and c.

2. The only exception to the marital exemption for sexual assault in Texas is if the husband and wife are living separately.

    a. True
    b. False

3. If the actor did not know that the victim was incapable of appraising the nature of the act because of a mental disease, the actor is still guilty of the crime of sexual assault.

    a. True
    b. False

4. If the actor, 22 years old, did not know that the victim was 16 years old and can show that the victim looked much older and lied about her age, he can be found guilty of sexual assault in Texas.

    a. True
    b. False

5. By arguing that he was not aware of her age, the defense offered by the actor in Question 4 is:

    a. mistake of law.
    b. mistake of fact.
    c. the victim was promiscuous.
    d. he was overwhelmed and acted in self-defense.

6. Margaret Jones was the Director of Public Parks for a medium sized city. She told the owner of a small business that did work for her department that unless he had sexual relations with her, she would make public that he had overcharged the city in a number of different transactions. The businessman submitted but afterwards decided to report the incident to the police. Jones can be found guilty of:

    a. nothing, the businessman was not threatened with force or violence and no weapons were used by Jones. He consented.
    b. he can sue her in civil court for sexual harassment but there is no criminal charge.
    c. sexual assault under section 22.011(b)(8).
    d. extortion.

7. A victim's uncorroborated testimony can be used against a defendant in a sexual assault case if the:

    a. victim made an outcry statement within one year of the crime.
    b. defendant made a confession to the crime.
    c. defendant had a prior history of sexual assault.
    d. victim's outcry statement specifically identifies the defendant as the actor.

8. A victim's prior sexual conduct can be introduced into a trial of a sexual assault crime if:

    a. under no condition; it is never admissible.
    b. the State introduces medical evidence and evidence of the victim's prior sexual conduct can rebut or explain it.
    c. it relates to past sexual conduct with the accused that relates to the issue of consent.
    d. b and c.

9. If Jack was 18 years old when he had consensual sexual relations with Lily who is 15 years old, he can still be found guilty of sexual assault because Lily is a child under section 22.011.

    a. True
    b. False

10. The crime of assault can be committed in Texas if a person:

    a. intentionally, knowingly or recklessly threatens another person with imminent bodily harm.
    b. intentionally threatens another with imminent bodily harm.
    c. intentionally or knowingly threatens another person with imminent bodily harm.
    d. recklessly threatens a person with imminent bodily harm.

11. In order for an assault to be aggravated, it must have resulted in serious injury to the victim.

    a. True
    b. False

12. Injury to an elderly person can occur:

    a. intentionally only.
    b. intentionally and knowingly.
    c. intentionally, knowingly and recklessly.
    d. intentionally, knowingly, recklessly and with criminal negligence.

13. Although no one was injured, Joe knowingly fired a firearm into a building he assumed was unoccupied because business hours had ended. Joe can be charged with:

    a. aggravated assault.
    b. deadly conduct.
    c. threatening the public.
    d. assault.

14. Tommy was angry with his boss because he did not receive a raise. Tommy wanted to scare his boss, so he took his unloaded pistol to his place of employment and waived it around while he yelled at his boss and threatened to harm him if things did not change. Tommy never laid a hand on his boss. Tommy can be charged with:

    a. assault only, no injuries occurred and the gun was not loaded.
    b. aggravated assault, the fact that there were no injuries and the gun was not loaded is not relevant.
    c. no crime, this was a disagreement only and Tommy never intended harm.
    d. deadly conduct for bringing a pistol into a building and exhibiting it.

15. The law of parties only applies to very serious offenses like homicide and sexual assault.

    a. True
    b. False

CHAPTER ELEVEN

CRIMES AGAINST HABITATION: BURGLARY AND ARSON

INTRODUCTION

Many of us have been the victims of a burglary or an attempted burglary. Our homes, places of business or automobiles have been broken into and the contents stolen. Those of us who live in large, urban areas may even be blasé about burglary to the point of not bothering to report a crime when the value of the stolen items was below the amount of the insurance deductible. We do not expect the police to capture the burglar much less recover our property. Criminal trespass and criminal mischief are also crimes we may chose to ignore if the damage was not significant or the circumstances were such that it was not worth the trouble of calling the police. On the other hand, a house burglary, especially, can seriously undermine our sense of security. A large industry caters to that insecurity: house and car alarm systems, gates, burglar bars, and breeders of large German Shepherds! We may feel uncertain about what to expect after discovering that someone has trespassed on out property or done damage to it. Burglary, criminal trespass, and criminal mischief crimes have residual effects that extend far beyond the actual damage done or loss incurred. This chapter begins by examining the Texas laws that address burglary and criminal trespass. It looks at arson, a crime that has become so complex in its execution that it requires the expertise of specially trained arson investigators. It ends with a review of the criminal mischief statutes.

BURGLARY

Prior to 1974, burglary was categorized into distinct offenses based on the burglar's time of entry. Under the former code, burglary of a private residence at night was a separate offense, which was penalized more severely than ordinary burglary. If the accused was charged with a daytime burglary, entry had to be effected by an actual breaking or by entry at an unusual place. If the charge was a nighttime burglary, evidence of an actual breaking was not essential, and proof of entry by force, threat, or fraud was sufficient. The 1974 code eliminated any distinction between daytime and nighttime burglary and omitted the breaking requirement.

The Burglary Statutes

Burglary is now defined in Section 30.02 of the Texas Penal Code. A person commits burglary if, without the effective consent of the owner, he:

(1) enters a habitation or building, or any portion of the building, not open to the public, with the intent to commit a felony, theft or an assault;

(2) remains concealed, with the intent to commit a felony, theft, or assault, in a building or a habitation; or

(3) enters a building or habitation and commits or attempts to commit a felony, theft, or an assault.

The punishment range for burglaries depends on the type of premises the burglar entered. If the premises were a habitation, it is a second-degree felony. Entry into a building is a state jail felony. Two circumstances can elevate a second-degree burglary of a habitation to a first-degree felony. If any party entered the habitation with the intent to commit a felony other than theft or committed or attempted to commit a felony other than felony theft, the punishment is first-degree.

Effective consent is defined as consent by a person legally authorized to act for the owner. Consent is not effective if it is based on fraud, force or threats. Effective consent cannot be given by someone who the defendant knows does not have authority because of age, mental disease or defect, or intoxication that has impaired his or her ability to make a decision.

The Entry Requirement

The crime of burglary is completed once the burglar enters the premises, whether or not any theft, felony, or assault was committed after the entry. The felony or theft does not have to be from the burglarized structure or from the owner of the structure. The State only needs to show that there was a clear connection between the unauthorized entry and the felony or theft. This is much broader than the common law of burglary that required the theft or felony be from or occur in the burglarized premises. For example, in *Robles v. State*, 664 S.W.2d 91 (Tex.Crim.App. 1984), the defendant broke into a home and forced the owner to accompany him to a bank where the owner obtained money for the intruder. Robles' burglary conviction was affirmed. The 1999 legislature added assault to the list of offenses that a burglar can intend to commit upon gaining entry to a habitation or building. Until Texas courts have the opportunity to address cases that raise tricky issues about what connection must exist between an unauthorized entry and an assault, prior cases law suggests the assault did not have to occur on the premises for a burglary to have been committed.

According to section 30.02, entry can be accomplished by the intrusion of any part of the body or any physical object connected to the body. A burglar is also someone who lawfully entered premises but remained concealed once the premises were closed if he or she had the intent to commit felony, theft, or assault. In *Ortega v. State*, 626 S.W.2d 746 (Tex.Crim.App. 1981), entry was affected when the defendant entered into a part of the house between the screen door and the wooden door. Where a defendant dug a hole though a roof with an automobile wrench, the intrusion of the wrench was an unlawful entry in *Hayes v. State*, 656 S.W.2d 926 (Tex. App. - Eastland 1983).

Habitations and Buildings

A habitation is defined in section 30.01 as a structure or vehicle that is adapted for the use of overnight accommodation of persons. It includes each separately secured or occupied portion of the structure or vehicle and each structure appurtenant to or connected with the structure or vehicle.

In 1976, the Court of Criminal Appeals ruled in *Jones v. State*, 532 S.W.2d 596 (Tex.Crim. App. 1976) that a habitation had to have been adapted for overnight accommodation prior to the burglary and still have been used for that purpose at the time of the offense. The *Jones* court ruled that a new home with no previous occupants, no furniture, and no utilities was not a habitation. In *Moss v. State*, 574 S.W.2d 542 (Tex.Crim.App. 1978), the Court of Criminal Appeals ruled that a furnished home that had been rented in the past but was unoccupied at the time of the burglary was a habitation. The court also ruled, however, that a house with past tenants and no utilities and which was being used for storage was not a habitation. In 1989, the Court of Criminal Appeals acknowledged that it needed to clarify the statute. It decided that the nature of the premises is defined by how an ordinary person would reasonably perceive it. In *Blankenship v. State*, 780 S.W.2d 198 (Tex.Crim.App. 1988), the Court ruled that a structure that had once been occupied, was rented occasionally, had functional rooms, connected utilities and was being used to store household items was a habitation for purposes of the burglary statute.

Garages and carports are considered parts of habitations because they are appurtenant to them. It does not matter whether they were opened or closed at the time of the burglary. Court cases have decided that appurtenant means any structure connected to the use and enjoyment of a habitation, including unattached garages, storage sheds, and other outbuildings. See *Jones v. State*, 690 S.W.2d 318 (Tex. App. - Dallas 1985).

"Buildings" are enclosed structures intended for use or occupation as a habitation or for some purpose of trade, manufacture, ornament, or use. In *Day v. State*, 534 S.W.2d 681 (Tex.Crim.App. 1976), the Court of Criminal Appeals considered a building that was made of concrete blocks, had three entries that could not be closed, and was surrounded by a fence. Because the structure was not enclosed, was not designed to secure its contents, and was permanently open, the court did not consider it to be a building. Being enclosed by something else, such as a fence, did not change the character of the structure.

Enclosed areas that are not open to the public are also considered buildings for purposes of the crime of burglary. If a defendant enters a public area but makes his way to a storage area or office that is closed to the general public with the intent to commit a felony, theft, or assault he or she is guilty of burglary.

Mens Rea

Entry must be accompanied with intent to commit a felony, theft, or assault when the offender enters a habitation or building under section 30.02(a)(1) and (2). Intent to commit a felony, theft, or assault is also required for a burglary committed by a surreptitious remaining. The intent must be present at the time of entry. If a defendant forms the intent after entering the premises, it is not a burglary. The circumstances surrounding a case are used to prove mens rea. The courts in Texas have ruled that it is permissible to infer that a nighttime entry included intent to commit a theft, felony, or assault. The State cannot rely on this inference in front of a jury, but a jury is permitted to make the inference according to *Browning v. State*, 720 S.W.2d 180 (Tex.Crim.App. 1986).

If a defendant is charged under section 30.02 (a)(3), there is no requirement that the entry was made with the intent to commit a felony, theft, or assault if the felony, theft, or assault was actually committed. All that is required is that the defendant enter the premises without the owner's consent and attempt to commit or commit a felony, theft, or assault. In *Davila v. State*, 547 S.W.2d 606 (Tex.Crim.App. 1977), the Texas Court of Criminal Appeals ruled that an unauthorized entry under subsection (a)(3) must be done intentionally or knowingly.

Other Burglary Statutes

Burglary of a motor vehicle is covered in a separate statute in section 30.04. The statute provides that a crime is committed if without the effective consent of the owner, a person breaks into or enters a vehicle or any part of a vehicle with the intent to commit any felony or theft. Intent to commit assault is not included. To enter means to intrude any part of the body or any physical object connected to the body. There is no requirement that the vehicle not be open to the public. Unlike burglary of a habitation or building, burglary of a vehicle still requires a breaking and entering. A use of force is necessary to establish the offense. Steeling tires, hubcaps or ornamentation on the outside of an automobile does not constitute burglary of a motor vehicle.

Section 30.03 defines the crime of Burglary of Coin-Operated or Coin Collection Machines. For purposes of the entry requirement, any entry without the effective consent of the owner is sufficient.

Exercises:
Probably the best and most interesting way to learn about the crime of burglary is to read actual cases decided by Texas courts. Below are a few to start, but you can find cases yourself.

Rogers v. State, 929 S.W.2d 103 (Tex. App. - Beaumont 1996): there was sufficient circumstantial evidence that the defendant entered a habitation to support his burglary conviction, based on his unexplained possession of recently stolen property and the circumstances of that possession. There was no evidence that anyone was ever seen entering or leaving the home, and no direct identification evidence.
Lawhorn v. State, 898 S.W.2d 886 (Tex.Crim.App. 1995): defendant was convicted of burglary of a habitation with intent to commit felony escape. The court ruled it was legally impossible for the defendant to have intended to commit the crime of escape when he unlawfully entered a habitation. The escape occurred when he left the custody of the police officer.
Soto v. State, 782 S.W.2d 17 (Tex. App. - San Antonio 1989): a locked toolbox bolted to the bed of a truck constituted "any part of the vehicle" and satisfied that element of burglary of a vehicle.
Mack v. State, 928 S.W.2d 219 (Tex. App. - Austin 1996): on the night of the burglary, the defendant's girlfriend had a greater right to possession of the apartment for which the two of them had signed a lease. She was the owner of the apartment within the meaning of the burglary statute. Defendant had stopped paying rent, had moved out, a new roommate was paying rent, and the defendant had agreed not to visit the apartment unless he first called for permission.
Richardson v. State, 888 S.W.2d 822 (Tex.Crim.App. 1994): an individual who reaches into the open bed of a pickup trick with the intent to remove property breaks into the close of the vehicle and enters part of the vehicle under section 30.04.
Van Dalen v. State, 789 S.W.2d 334 (Tex. App. - Houston [14th Dist.] 1990): the fact that a truck was without a motor or rear wheels did not destroy its character as a vehicle under section 30.04.
Jones v. State, 899 S.W.2d 25 (Tex. App. - Tyler 1995): evidence that missing property was found in defendant's truck on the same day it was taken and when confronted, the defendant did not offer to explain his possession or return the property, was sufficient for burglary of a habitation. His vehicle matched the description of a vehicle seen earlier on the day of the crime.

CRIMINAL TRESPASS

An unauthorized entry into another person's premises, including an aircraft, is the crime of criminal trespass. Defined in section 30.05 of the Penal Code, it is almost identical to burglary except that there is no intent to commit a felony, theft, or assault. The statute requires that the defendant either had notice that entry was forbidden or received notice to depart. Under subsection (a)(2), notice is satisfied in four different ways:

(A) if the owner or someone acting under the owner's authority provided written or oral communication;
(B) fencing or other enclosure was erected around the premises;
(C) signs were posted forbidding entry on the property;
(D) the visible presence of a crop grown for human consumption that is under cultivation, being harvested, or marketable if already harvested.

Unlike burglary, criminal trespass requires entry of the entire body. Entry of a part of the body or a physical object connected to the body is insufficient.

It is a defense to prosecution that at the time of the entry, the actor was a fire fighter or emergency medical service personnel acting according to official duties. Criminal trespass is a Class B misdemeanor unless it was committed in a habitation, shelter center or a Superfund site, or if the defendant carried a deadly weapon during the criminal trespass. In those cases, it is a Class A misdemeanor.

The 1999 Texas legislature added two new provisions to the criminal trespass statutes. One makes it criminal to enter an aircraft without the owner's consent. The second provision makes it criminal trespass to enter or remain on agricultural land without the express consent of the owner or other legal authorization. To be guilty of the crime, the offender must have been on notice that entry was forbidden or fail to depart when asked to and be on the land when apprehended or within 100 feet of the land's boundary.

ARSON

Section 28.02 of the Penal Code defines the crime of arson. It prohibits starting a fire or setting an explosion with intent to destroy or do damage to any building, habitation, or vehicle. A recent amendment to the arson statute recognizes that setting a fire to agricultural land can cause economic damage. Arson now includes setting a fire to destroy or damage any vegetation, fence, or structure on open-space land. Open-space land is real property undeveloped for human habitation.

The statute requires under subsection (a)(2) that when the charge concerns setting a fire to a building, habitation, or vehicle, there be a showing the actor knew the premises:

(A) was within the limits of an incorporated city or town;
(B) was insured against damage or destruction;
(C) was subject to a mortgage or other security interest;
(D) was located on property belonging to another person;

(E) had located within it property of another person; or
(F) when the defendant was reckless about whether the burning or explosion would endanger the life of another or the safety of the property of another.

Subsection (a)(2)(A) recognizes that intentionally setting a fire inside a city's limits can be more dangerous than setting a fire in more remote areas. Under (a)(2)(B), the State must prove that the fire was set for the purpose of collecting the insurance benefits. *Miller v. State*, 566 S.W.2d 614 (Tex.Crim.App. 1978). Subsection (a)(2)(E) protects a person who owns property located on premises he or she does not own. The statute also makes clear that an owner, under certain specific circumstances, can set fire to his or her own property and be guilty of arson.

Arson is a second-degree felony unless injury or death occurs because of the offense, in which case it is a felony of the first-degree. In many cases, a death that occurs because of an arson offense can be prosecuted as a felony capital murder. The difference between a capital murder charge and first-degree felony arson is that in capital murder the State must prove the defendant knew the existence of a potential victim. This is because the State must show the defendant committed an act clearly dangerous to human life while in the course of committing an underlying felony. With arson, a defendant can be convicted of first-degree felony without having to be aware that someone could be killed or was killed. If he or she committed arson to collect the insurance proceeds without knowing that someone was inside the premises, they are guilty of first-degree felony arson.

Prior to 1974, a building had to be damaged for the crime of arson to occur. Since 1974, the starting of a fire or causing an explosion is sufficient. There need be no actual damage. It makes no difference if the property was constructed of inflammable material. If the defendant intended to do damage, the crime was committed.

CRIMINAL MISCHIEF

Section 28.03 defines the crime of criminal mischief. When it was enacted in 1974, section 28.03 replaced forty separate offenses. It addresses the intentional and knowing destruction of property. Section 28.04, Reckless Damage or Destruction, is aimed at reckless destruction of property. The two offenses combined forbid all damage to property, except arson, regardless of how it was inflicted or the nature of the property harmed.

Criminal mischief and reckless damage include damaging or destroying property, tampering with property and causing pecuniary loss or substantial inconvenience to the owner, and making markings, slogans, drawings, or paintings on property. The punishment range for the crime is based on the value of the property that was damaged or its cost of repair.

- Class C misdemeanor - damage of $50 or less;
- Class B misdemeanor - damage of $50 to $500;
- Class A misdemeanor - damage of $500 to $1500;
- State jail felony - damage of $1500 to $20,000;
- Third-degree felony - damage of $20,000 to $100,000;
- Second-degree felony - damage of $100,00 to $200,000;
- First-degree felony - damage of $200,000 or more.

The Texas legislature frequently adjusts these value limits. The statute makes it a crime to impair, interrupt, or divert public communications, transportation, water, gas, power supply, or any public service. It is also a state jail felony to damage or destroy a place of worship, human burial grounds, a public monument, or a community center and the loss is less than $20,000. The reckless damage or destruction of property is a Class C misdemeanor, regardless of the amount of reckless damage or the cost of repair.

> **Exercises:**
> Read section 28.06 in the Penal Code to understand how the amount of pecuniary loss is calculated. This can become an important issue in a case because the seriousness of the punishment is based on these calculations. The statute is careful to outline criteria for determining loss. It is up to the State and the defense to argue the details. Issues involving the amount of loss may require the testimony of experts whose profession it is to appraise the value of property. Notice the statute only protects against pecuniary loss. Emotional and psychological loss have no role in the criminal arena. A conviction for criminal mischief does not preclude a civil lawsuit for damages.
>
> Section 28.07, Interference with Railroad Property, was made an offense by the Texas legislature in 1989.

FINAL COMMENTS ON CRIMES AGAINST HABITATIONS

The crimes of burglary, arson, and criminal trespass cover a lot of conduct. They have become more and more inclusive over the centuries as our style of living has changed. Homes are enhanced with garages, storage sheds, and barns. We spend significant time in our vehicles where we keep valuable personal property. There is little difference between daytime and nighttime in a society that functions 24 hours a day. Our property is often insured and mortgaged, giving persons other than owners a financial stake in its well-being. Changes in how we live and do business are evident in the evolution of property offenses.

MULTIPLE CHOICE QUESTIONS

1. Johnny, 17 years old, was caught scribbling graffiti on the outside walls of his high school. It cost $155.00 to remove the graffiti. Johnny can be charged with:

    a. he can be expelled, but no criminal charges can be brought against him.
    b. a Class A misdemeanor because it was a public building.
    c. a Class B misdemeanor.
    d. a Class C misdemeanor based on his reckless behavior.

2. Simon decided to burglarize a local video store and steal all of his favorite movies. He drove his truck into the front window of the store. The police found him in his truck passed out from the collision before he could enter the store. The truck smashed the window and shattered it. Simon argued he is not guilty of burglarizing the store because he never entered it. Is his defense valid?

a. Yes, he never entered the store.
   b. No, his truck entered the store sufficiently for the crime of burglary.
   c. Yes, he never stole items from the store.
   d. No, he satisfied the burglary statute's breaking requirement.

3. Mr. Grumble posted signs all over his house and yard telling people to stay off his property. Some of his less mature neighbors were tired of his unneighborly ways and decided to teach him a lesson. They threw basketballs into his yard on a regular basis to annoy him. The balls did no damage to his yard. He went to the D.A. and filed a complaint. The D.A. explained that:

   a. the neighbors can be charged with criminal trespass.
   b. the neighbors cannot be charged with criminal trespass because they did not enter his property.
   c. the neighbors can be charged with criminal mischief.
   d. both b and c.

4. Johnson decided to burn down an old shed on his property outside of town. He doused it with gasoline and it burned. Unfortunately, the wind was blowing wildly that day, and the shed was close to his barn. The barn burned down also. The barn was subject to a bank mortgage. Can Johnson be found guilty of arson?

   a. Yes, he was reckless and property was destroyed that the bank had an interest in.
   b. No, you cannot be guilty of arson for destroying your own property.
   c. No, the property was located outside town limits.
   d. Yes, he was intentionally destroyed his shed and that intent is transferred to his barn.

5. The thief who tried to steal Carrie's very expensive car radio and sound system ($2500 cost) was caught and convicted. Luckily Carrie had an alarm, but the damage to the sound system was extensive - at least $1500. He had no prior offenses. He faced a Class A burglary misdemeanor charge.

   a. True
   b. False

6. Two roommates shared an apartment with the understanding that their bedrooms were totally off limits to each other. One of the roommates came home to find the other roommate in his bedroom, looking through his dresser drawers. In his pocket, he had an expensive ring that he had found in the dresser drawer. Can the snoopy roommate be charged with burglary?

   a. No, they share an apartment together.
   b. No, the bedrooms are not separate habitations.
   c. Yes, the bedrooms are separately occupied and the entry was without consent.
   d. No, he had not yet left the apartment with the ring.

7. Tony set fire to Angela's house because in her front room she had a grand piano that had belonged to Tony's famous pianist father. Angela won the piano from Tony in a poker game. Tony was heartbroken and decided that if he could not have the piano; no one should have it. He did not intend to destroy Angela's house. His intent was to destroy the piano by setting fire to the house. Luckily, the fire was stopped before any damage was done to Angela's home. Is Tony guilty of arson?

    a. No, he did not intend to destroy the house.
    b. No, because there was no damage to the home.
    c. Yes, he intended to start a fire and did start a fire.
    d. Yes, Angela's house was in the city limits.

8. Before being caught by the police for setting fire to Angela's house, Tony decided to break into Angela's house and destroy the piano with a sledgehammer. He attended a party at her home but failed to leave after all the other guests left. Angela went to bed, thinking everyone had gone home. Tony was secreted in a closet. While Angela slept, he destroyed the piano. Tony is guilty of:

    a. criminal mischief only.
    b. burglary.
    c. criminal trespass and reckless damage to property.
    d. criminal trespass.

9. Before Tony acted on his design to destroy Angela's newly won piano; he went to a psychotherapist who convinced him not to take revenge. He attended a party at Angela's home and got very intoxicated. He leaned against the famous piano against Angela's warnings to stay away from it. In his drunken stupor, he pounded on the keyboard and damaged several keys. It was expensive to repair. Tony can be charged with:

    a. nothing, let Angela sue him in civil court.
    b. reckless damage or destruction to property.
    c. criminal mischief.
    d. no crime because the damage cannot be calculated.

10. Tony is obsessed with his father's piano. He broke into Angela's home one evening while she was not there to play the piano for several hours. He left Angela a note thanking her for a wonderful evening. Angela was furious because she had told Tony repeatedly to stay away from her home. Tony can be charged with:

    a. burglary, he broke into Angela's home.
    b. criminal mischief.
    c. criminal trespass.
    d. give him a break, he's a sad guy.

CHAPTER TWELVE

CRIMES AGAINST PROPERTY

INTRODUCTION

Chapter 31 of the Texas Penal Code, which defines theft offenses, is by far the broadest, most comprehensive set of statutes in the Code. Some of the theft offenses are based on the value of the property taken. Others focus on the type of property taken, and others on the manner in which the property was taken. Robbery is defined in sections 29.02 and 29.03 of the Code. Fraud, including forgery crimes, is defined in Chapter 32. This chapter will primarily examine theft, robbery, and forgery with a brief look at other fraud offenses.

THEFT

Prior to 1974, Texas courts spent a considerable amount of time in theft cases deciding exactly what type of theft occurred and whether the State charged the defendant with the correct crime. The legislature addressed those problems when it created a consolidated theft statute. In section 31.02, the lawmakers made clear that theft is theft is theft in Texas. All theft crimes were consolidated into one main statute - section 31.03. No longer are larceny, shoplifting, embezzlement, false pretenses, extortion, receiving or concealing stolen property, or conversion by a bailee defined as different offenses. There were only two made exceptions in 1974. The legislature created a separate statute for theft of services and for the unauthorized use of an automobile.

The Theft Statute

A person commits theft if he or she unlawfully appropriates property with the intent to deprive the owner of the property. Appropriation is unlawful if it:

(1) is without the effective consent of the owner;
(2) the property is stolen and the defendant appropriates the property knowing it was stolen; or
(3) property in the custody of a law enforcement agency was explicitly represented to the defendant as being stolen and the defendant appropriates the property believing it was stolen.

The mens rea of the crime of theft is the intent to deprive the owner of property. Section 31.01 defines the terms "appropriate," "deprive," "effective consent," "property," "deception," and "service." These definitions are essential for understanding the crime of theft.

"Deprive" is defined as to withhold property from the owner permanently or for an extended period of time so that a major portion of the property's value or enjoyment is lost to the owner. "Deprive" also means to restore property only upon payment of a reward or compensation or to dispose of property in a way that makes its recovery unlikely. Intent to deprive often becomes an issue if the defendant asserts he exercised control over the property for only a short while. Prior to 1974, the statute required that the defendant permanently intend to deprive the owner of property. Under the consolidated statute, the State can now show that the owner was deprived for a period of time in a manner that interfered with using or enjoying the property. It is the defendant's intent at the time the property was taken that must be established. If a defendant takes property with the intent of keeping it permanently and later decides to return it, he or she can still face theft charges.

The actus reus of theft is to unlawfully appropriate someone else's property. "Appropriate" is defined as to bring about the transfer of title or other nonpossessory interest in property to the defendant or to another person or to acquire or otherwise exercise control over the property.

The Texas Court of Criminal Appeals interpreted the meaning of "intent to deprive" in *McClain v. State*, 687 S.W.2d 350 (Tex.Crim.App. 1985). The court ruled that if a defendant exercised control over the owner's property knowing they did not have the owner's consent and with the intent to deprive the owner, the defendant committed theft. The crime of theft was accomplished without regard to how the defendant acquired the property. This ruling has made it easier for the State to establish both the mens rea and actus reus elements of theft.

Section 31.06 permits the presumption that the defendant intended to steal property or services if he or she obtained them by issuing or passing a check when there were insufficient funds on deposit with the bank for the full payment of the check. This presumption operates under one of two conditions: if the defendant had no account at the bank at the time he or she issued the check or payment was refused by the bank because of insufficient funds and the defendant failed to pay the holder of the check within 10 days after receiving notice.

Exercise:
Read the definition of effective consent in section 31.01. Read the definition of coercion in section 1.07. The two statutes have to be read together in order to understand fully what is effective consent. In the majority of theft cases, it is not difficult to establish that the owner did not consent to a taking of his or her property. Locate cases where the facts suggest that the issue of effective consent was central to the case.

Receiving Stolen Property

Prior to 1974, receiving stolen property and concealing stolen property were two separate offenses. The new Code consolidated those offenses into the general theft offense. Technically, there is no offense of receiving stolen property. The crime is appropriating property that the defendant knows is stolen. The statute provides that evidence of similar and recent offenses to the current charge can be admitted in order to establish knowledge that the property was stolen. An accomplice's uncorroborated testimony can be introduced to establish both knowledge and intent.

Finally, section 31.03 permits certain presumptions to be made. A person who is in the business of selling used merchandise is presumed to know the property was stolen if he or she pays more than $25.00 for it and fails to record the seller's name, address, physical description or identification number, fails to record a complete description of the property, including serial number or fails to obtain a warranty from the seller that the seller has the right to possess the property. Legal presumptions are governed by section 2.05 of the Penal Code. Presumptions are a powerful leverage for the State. If there is sufficient evidence of the facts required to establish a presumption, the issue is submitted to the jury. The jury, however, is instructed that the facts establishing the presumption must be proved beyond a reasonable doubt, and that they are not obligated to accept the presumption.

> **Exercise:**
> Take note that section 30.03 also includes special provisions for persons who buy and sell second-hand automobiles and pesticides. Until 1993, the statute also provided that persons who possessed shopping carts away from the store premises were presumed to know the property belonged to the store.

Punishment

The value of the stolen property is the primary determinant of punishment for a theft crime. Punishment can range from a Class C to a first-degree felony. Punishment ranges are amended by the legislature periodically. Section 31.08 provides the standards by which value is to be calculated.

In some instances, the character of the property determines the punishment range. Theft of livestock is determined by both the value of the livestock and the number of animals stolen. Theft of property from another person or from a human corpse or grave is a state jail felony, regardless of the property's value. Stealing from a person using force or violence would be a robbery, not a theft. Picking pockets and purse snatching, however, are covered by the theft statute. *Cook v. State*, 706 S.W.2d 775 (Tex. App. – Houston [14th Dist.] 1986). If the stolen property was a firearm, it is also punished as a state jail felony. Until the 1993 legislative amendments, theft of oil field equipment, oil, and natural gas was a second-degree felony, regardless of the value.

If public servant appropriated property by virtue of his or her status as a public servant, punishment is increased to the next higher category.

Section 31.09 allows the State to aggregate a number of thefts together and prosecute them as one criminal offense. As long as the State can show that the thefts resulted from one scheme or continuing course of conduct, the conduct can be considered one crime and the amounts stolen can be aggregated for determining punishment.

In *Hardesty v. State*, 656 S.W.2d 73 (Tex.Crim.App. 1983), the Court of Criminal Appeals ruled that if a defendant is found in possession of stolen property and offers no reasonable explanation for his or her possession, a jury may infer that the defendant stole the property. If the inference is used, there must be evidence that the property found with the defendant is the same as the property that was stolen. The property must be in the defendant's exclusive possession and had to be recently stolen. The *Hardesty* inference is not available for crimes involving receiving stolen property where it must be established that the defendant knew the property was stolen.

Theft of Service

Section 31.04 defines theft of service. Service is generally anything that would be provided for compensation that would not be considered property, such as labor, professional services, and rental of property. Labor is not always a service if it was primarily the property the defendant was seeking to gain. There are situations that are mixed service/property transactions. Are you purchasing food - property, or service - food preparation - in a restaurant? Courts typically apply the theft of service statute when some service was intended. Restaurant food and hotel rooms are considered services. *Chance v. State*, 579 S.W.2d 471 (Tex.Crim.App. 1979).

Theft of service can occur in three ways if the defendant intended to avoid payment for service he knew were provided for compensation:

(1) intentionally or knowingly securing service by deception, threat, or false token;
(2) intentionally or knowingly diverting services of another to one's own or another's benefit;
(3) failing to return rental property after the expiration of the written rental agreement period.

Intent to avoid payment can be presumed if:

(1) the defendant absconded without making payment or expressly refused to pay in a situation in which payment is typically made when the service is rendered, as in hotels, campgrounds, recreational vehicle parks, and restaurants;
(2) the defendant failed to return rental property within 10 days after receiving notice demanding payment;
(3) the defendant returned rental property but failed to pay the rental charge for the property within 10 days of receiving notice demanding payment.

If the State attempts to show the defendant absconded without making payment, there must be evidence that he or she left clandestinely or furtively. It is not sufficient that he or she simply left without making payment. *Manly v. State*, 622 S.W.2d 881 (Tex.Crim.App. 1982). The importance of the deception element was emphasized in *Bullet v. State*, 538 S.W.2d 785 (Tex.Crim.App. 1976). In that case the maid, who had been instructed not to make long distance telephone calls on her employer's phone, was found not to have committed theft of service by accepting a collect call on that phone because there was no showing of deception.

> **Exercises:**
> Chapter 31 of the Penal Code includes several other theft offenses that were added by the Texas legislature since 1974. Theses more specific theft offenses would be interesting to research. How are these laws enforced? How frequently do they result in prosecutions? How has the law developed in these areas?
>
> Section 31.05 - Theft of Trade Secrets
> Section 31.11 - Tampering with Identification Numbers
> Section 31.12 - Unauthorized Use of Television Decoding and Interception Device or Cable Descrambling, Decoding, or Interception Device
> Section 31.13 - Manufacture, Sale, or Distribution of Television Decoding and Interception Device or Cable Descrambling, or Interception Device.

Unauthorized Use of a Motor Vehicle

Unauthorized use of a motor vehicle is defined in section 31.07. Included as motor vehicles are automobiles, trucks, boats, airplanes, and any other motor-propelled vehicle. The section makes it unlawful intentionally or knowingly to operate another person's motor vehicle without their consent. "Operate" means to drive the vehicle. There are limits on the extent to which circumstantial evidence can be used to show operation. In *Anthony v. State*, 628 S.W.2d 151 (Tex. App. - Houston [14th Dist.] 1982), the court held that even though the defendant was seen exiting the driver's seat in a car and fleeing the scene when approached by a police officer who testified that the car could not have been turned off for more than two minutes, there was insufficient evidence of unauthorized use of the vehicle.

In *Lynch v. State*, 643 S.W.2d 737 (Tex.Crim.App. 1983), the Court of Criminal Appeals ruled that the mistake of fact defense is limited to those situations in which a defendant claimed he or she had a third party's permission to operate the vehicle. The Court of Criminal Appeals has also held that the State must prove the defendant knew he or she did not have the owner's consent. *Gardner v. State*, 780 S.W.2d 259 (Tex.Crim.App. 1989).

> **Exercises:**
> Read *Hudson v. State*, 510 S.W.2d 583 (Tex.Crim.App. 1974) and *Dickson v. State*, 642 S.W.2d 185 (Tex. App. - Houston [14th Dist.] 1982) for further illustrations of what "operate" means in section 31.07. In both cases, the courts refused to find that the defendants had operated a motor vehicle. The cases demonstrate how limited the use of circumstantial evidence is in proving this crime. Why do you think Texas courts have made it so difficult to prove operation for the purposes of convicting someone of the unauthorized use of a motor vehicle? Circumstantial evidence is often sufficient in proving up elements of other offenses.
>
> In contrast, read *Denton v. State*, 880 S.W.2d 255 (Tex. App. – Fort Worth 1994), which upheld the defendant's conviction for unauthorized use of a motor vehicle. The defendant attempted to steal a truck that would not run until it had warmed up for at least five minutes. The truck owner stopped the defendant before the truck had warmed up. The court concluded the defendant had exerted enough power, influence and control over the truck to constitute operation.

FRAUD

Chapter 32 defines crimes involving fraudulent conduct. Common to all the offenses in the chapter is fraudulent intent. Crimes of fraud do not require a victim who has suffered harm. If a defendant acts in fraudulent conduct with the intent defined in the statute, the defendant can be prosecuted even if no one has suffered loss. Section 32.01 defines the terms common to the fraud crimes, including "financial institution," "property," "service," and "steal." Section 32.02 sets out the manner for determining the value of stolen property. Section 32.03 allows for the aggregation of amounts of property stolen as part of the same scheme or continuing course of conduct.

Forgery

Forgery is defined in section 32.21. There are three different types:

(1) to alter, make, complete, execute, or authenticate any writing so that it purports:
  a) to be the act of another who did not authorize that act;
  b) to have been executed at a time or place or in a numbered sequence other than what was in fact the case
  c) to be a copy of an original when no original existed
(2) to issue, transfer, register the transfer of, pass, publish, or otherwise utter a writing that has been forged
(3) to possess a writing that is forged with the intent to utter it

In short, forgery is making a forged instrument, passing a forged instrument, or possessing a forged instrument with the intent to utter. Depending on the nature of the forged writing, punishment for forgery can range from a Class A misdemeanor to third-degree felony.

The mens rea required by the statute is the intent to defraud or harm another person. Texas law prior to 1974 required only intent to defraud. By adding intent to harm as a second mens rea element, the legislature expanded the scope of the statute. According to *Landry v. State*, 583 S.W.2d 620 (Tex.Crim.App. 1979), the State no longer needs to establish that the defendant obtained property or received some benefit for the forged writing. If there was intent to harm someone, that is sufficient to satisfy the mens rea element. Under prior law, without a showing of harm, the case would be one of attempted forgery.

What constitutes a "writing" is broadly defined. Under prior Texas law, the forged instrument must have resulted in a pecuniary loss or somehow affected property. Since 1974, writings include symbols of value, right, privilege, or identification along with instruments and items that involve pecuniary obligations. Under the prior law, the forged instrument had to appear so genuine on its face that it would deceive a person under ordinary observation. The current statute is focused entirely on the defendant's intent. If the intent was to defraud, it does not matter that the forged instrument did not appear genuine.

Texas courts have made a distinction between a document signed by a third person using the signature of another person, which is considered forgery, and a document signed by a person authorized to sign but containing a false promise that does not affect the document's authenticity, which is not considered forgery. It is the document's deceptive appearance that creates forgery, not false statements within the document. *Sales v. State*, 628 S.W.2d 796 (Tex.Crim.App. 1982).

Criminal Simulation

Criminal simulation, defined in section 32.22, is almost the same as a forgery offense except it addresses objects and not writings. The mens rea is the same as forgery: intent to defraud or harm another person. The actus reus is to make or alter objects so that they appear to have value because of age, antiquity, rarity, source, or authorship. Like forgery, the actus reus element can be satisfied by possessing such an object with the intent to sell or pass it. It can also be satisfied by authenticating or certifying such an object as genuine or as different from what it is. There is no requirement that the defendant receive anything of value for the crime to have been committed.

Exercises:
Chapter 32 defines many other fraud offenses in addition to forgery and criminal simulation, such as:
Section 32.31 - Credit Card or Debit Card Abuse
Section 32,32 - False Statement to Obtain Property or Credit
Section 32.33 - Hindering Secured Creditors
Section 32.34 - Fraudulent Transfer of a Motor Vehicle
Section 32.35 - Credit Card Transaction Record Laundering
Section 32.41 - Issuance of Bad Check
Section 32.42 - Deceptive Business Practices
Section 32.43 - Commercial Bribery
Section 32.44 - Rigging Publicly Exhibited Contest
Section 32.441 - Illegal Recruitment of an Athlete
Section 32.45 - Misapplication of Fiduciary Property or Property of Financial Institution
Section 32.46 - Securing Execution of Document by Deception
Section 32.47 - Fraudulent Destruction, Removal, or Concealment of Writing

Review the elements of these crimes. Identify the mens rea and actus reus. Review some court cases that have interpreted the statutes. What distinguishes the offenses and what do they have in common? Contact your District Attorney's office about the prosecution of fraud offenses. Are they handled by a special division or assigned to special prosecutors?

Check with the Texas Attorney General's Office about the Texas Deceptive Trade Practices Act, which is enforced by that office and by private individuals. The Act allows for civil lawsuits to be filed for damages resulting from deceptive trade practices.

ROBBERY

Robbery and aggravated robbery are defined in Chapter 29. Robbery is a crime of violence and case law emphasizes the violent nature of the act. A person commits robbery under section 29.02 if, in the course of committing a theft and with the intent to obtain property or to maintain control over property, he or she:

(1) intentionally, knowingly, or recklessly causes injury to another person; or
(2) intentionally or knowingly threatens or places another person in fear of imminent injury or death.

If the evidence shows the defendant was reasonably certain that his or her conduct was likely to cause injury or they disregarded a known risk that their conduct would cause injury, the State has satisfied the requirements of (1). In *Lane v. State*, 763 S.W.2d 785 (Tex.Crim.App. 1989), the defendant snatched a purse off the arm of an undercover police officer posing as a stranded motorist. A struggle ensued over the purse, the defendant twisted the officer's wrist, and the officer sustained a bruise. The defendant argued he did not intentionally or knowingly injure the officer. The Court of Criminal Appeals ruled that in struggling with the officer and twisting her arm to obtain the purse, there was sufficient evidence that he was reasonably certain he would cause her injury. It is not necessary that the defendant inflict serious harm to a victim. The severity of the violence is not important as long as the victim suffered some physical pain, illness, or any impairment of physical condition. *Lewis v. State*, 530 S.W.2d 117 (Tex.Crim.App. 1975).

Injury and Threats

To prove that a defendant committed a robbery with threats of injury or death requires the State to prove the victim feared imminent injury and the fear was produced either intentionally or knowingly. The evidence must show that the victim was afraid because of the defendant's acts, conduct, or words. The defendant's acts, conduct, or words must be such that they would induce an ordinary person to part with their property.

The threat of imminent injury does not have to be verbal. Acts can threaten; such as by displaying a weapon or causing the victim to believe the attacker has a weapon. In *Patterson v. State*, 639 S.W.2d 695 (Tex.Crim.App. 1982), the defendant created the impression that he had a gun by holding his hand across his waist, as if the conceal it. The court found sufficient evidence that the defendant created an environment of fear in order to induce the victim to hand over his property. In *Hernandez v. State*, 656 S.W.2d 630 (Tex. App. – San Antonio 1983), the victim testified at trial he was not afraid during the attack, even though the defendant stabbed him in order to accomplish the theft. The court upheld the robbery conviction and found that despite the victim's testimony the defendant's conduct was so violent that only an unreasonable person would not have been afraid. In *Birl v. State*, 763 S.W.2d 860 (Tex.Crim.App. 1982), the defendant walked alongside the victim and displayed a knife. She screamed and ran away, dropping her purse. The defendant chased her, picked up her purse, and returned to his car. The court found the threats sufficient for a robbery conviction.

The injuries or threats must have been committed during the course of committing the theft. Section 29.01 defines "in the course of committing theft" as conduct that occurs in an attempt to commit, during the commission, or in immediate flight after the attempt or the commission of theft. Prior to 1974, the penal code required a completed theft in order to prove the crime of robbery. The definition of "in the course of committing theft" broadens the crime considerably. The violence, which is now the focus of the offense, can occur at any point during the criminal episode. It is not relevant whether the theft was completed or the property abandoned after it was taken. In *Yarbrough v. State*, 656 S.W.2d 200 (Tex. App. – Austin 1983), the court found robbery had been committed based on the fact that the defendant kicked the victim while trying to escape even though he had abandoned all attempts to secure the property. In *Thomas v. State*, 708 S.W.2d 580 (Tex. App. – Eastland 1986), the defendant was arrested for shoplifting. Fifteen or twenty minutes later, she tried to escape and inflicted injuries on a security guard in the process. The court concluded there was sufficient evidence of robbery.

Aggravated Robbery

Aggravated robbery is defined in section 29.03 of the Penal Code. There are three factors that can aggravate a simple robbery:

(1) causing serious bodily injury to another person;
(2) using or exhibiting a deadly weapon; or
(3) causing bodily injury or threatening imminent injury to a person who is 65 years or older or disabled.

It is not necessary that the defendant display the entire weapon, nor that the victim actually see the weapon. The court upheld an aggravated robbery conviction in *Benavidez v. State*, 670 S.W.2d 297 (Tex. App. – Amarillo 1983), based on facts that showed the defendant poked something into the victim's back that felt like a gun.

Robbery is a second-degree felony, and aggravated robbery is a first-degree felony.

FINAL COMMENTS ON CRIMES AGAINST PROPERTY

Crimes against property constitute a considerable portion of the work of law enforcement agencies and district attorneys' offices. They are complex crimes to define. The Texas theft statute is long and involved. Over the years, the legislature has added new theft crimes to address special circumstances.

Fraud crimes are also complex. The mens rea element is often difficult to prove beyond a reasonable doubt. For that reason, many fraudulent schemes are more easily handled as civil fraud. The victim sues the perpetrator of the fraud in civil court for civil damages. In civil court, proof is based on a preponderance of the evidence. The perpetrator is not subject to criminal punishment, but he or she can be ordered to make the victim whole and, in some circumstances, pay a punitive judgment beyond the amount of the victim's injuries.

In most respects, robbery is not a crime against property. It is a crime of violence against other persons committed during a theft. Since 1974, the Texas robbery statutes have treated robbery as a violent offense, more in the nature of assault, than as a property offense.

MULTIPLE CHOICE QUESTIONS

1. Sally operated a pawnshop in Houston. She regularly purchased items from Tommy who would bring in all kinds of merchandise. She was suspicious but liked the merchandise he sold her. She failed to get a warranty from him that he had the right to possess the property he sold. The police visit sally one day after Tommy is busted for burglary and selling the property he stole.

    a. She has nothing to worry about because she has no proof the merchandise was stolen.
    b. Sally faces a legal presumption that she knew the property was stolen.
    c. She has no problems because she was not a part of a burglary ring.
    d. She has problems only if Tommy implicates her.

2. The neighborhood Gang of Vandals forced small business owners on their block to pay them protection money. Failure to pay the money put the businesses at risk for being vandalized by gang members. The Vandals were apprehended by the Dallas police and charged with:

    a. extortion.
    b. theft.
    c. robbery.
    d. larceny.

3. Kevin "borrowed" his uncle's car because his car was in the shop and he had a date to impress. Unfortunately, Kevin did not request permission from his uncle, nor did he inform his uncle that he borrowed his car. Kevin intended to return the car that evening. Kevin has committed:

    a. theft of automobile.
    b. there was no crime because it involved another family member.
    c. unauthorized use of a motor vehicle.
    d. larceny.

4. Rocky Heartless, of Heartless Roofing Co., promised elderly Mrs. Smith that he would repair her roof for only $15,000.00, one-half of her life savings. He told her the roof would cave in if she did not act quickly. Mrs. Smith paid the money. As it turned out, the roof did not need any repair. Heartless is guilty of:

    a. nothing, let the buyer beware.
    b. theft.
    c. false pretenses.
    d. deceptive business practices.

5. Hanna Heartless, Rocky's sister and owner of Hanna H. Antiques, told Mrs. Smith that the armoire she purchased from Hanna dated from the early 1700s. In reality, the armoire dated to 1955. To be guilty of a crime, there must be proof that Hanna:

    a. altered the armoire to make it look older.
    b. bought the armoire from someone else who altered it.
    c. recklessly suggested the armoire was older than it really was.
    d. authenticated the armoire as from the 1700s with the intent to defraud Mrs. Smith.

6. Leroy decided to create false passports for his friends so they could take a quick trip to South America. He was not compensated by them, but provided his services as a favor. Leroy is guilty of a:

    a. third-degree felony.
    b. first-degree felony.
    c. Class A misdemeanor.
    d. b or c depending on the number of passports he made.

7. Sydney brandished a toy gun during his robbery of a convenience store. He had no other weapon with him, caused no injury, and never threatened verbally to hurt the store clerk who was the only other person in the store. Sydney cannot be convicted of aggravated robbery because the gun was not real.

    a. True
    b. False

8. The store clerk in the convenience store testified at trial that she knew the gun was a toy because her son has one just like it. She testified she was not afraid that Sydney would harm her. The clerk's testimony does not affect the aggravated robbery case against Sydney.

    a. True
    b. False

9. The store clerk was 70 years old. Sydney's arguments against aggravated robbery are unaffected by that fact.

    a. True
    b. False

10. Rocky Heartless not only ripped off Mrs. Smith but several other homeowners in her neighborhood as well, all within the same month for about $15,000.00 each. The D.A. can aggregate all the amounts involved in the fraud to determine Heartless's punishment.

    a. True
    b. False

CHAPTER THIRTEEN

CRIMES AGAINST PUBLIC ORDER AND MORALS

INTRODUCTION

This chapter looks at crimes against public order as defined by the Texas Penal Code, which are found primarily in Chapters 42. Public order offenses account for a high percentage of local law enforcement's workload, however, they generate few appellate court opinions. Sentenced for misdemeanors, persons convicted of crimes public order crimes generally do not appeal their cases. Many of these state offenses have counterparts in city and county ordinances.

DISORDERLY CONDUCT

Section 42.01 is a collection of less serious offenses under the label of disorderly conduct. The legislature periodically amends the list of twelve acts that make up the offense. They constitute the actus reus of the offense:

(1) using abusive, indecent, profane, or vulgar language in a public place and the language tends to incite a breach of the peace
(2) making an offensive gesture or display in a public place and the gesture tends to incite a breach of the peace
(3) creating through a chemical means a noxious and unreasonable odor in a public place
(4) abusing or threatening a person in a public place in an offensive manner
(5) making unreasonable noise in a public place or in or near a private residence that he has no right to occupy
(6) fighting with another person in a public place
(7) looking into the dwelling of another person for a lewd or unlawful purpose
(8) looking into another person's guest room at a hotel or comparable establishment for lewd or unlawful purposes
(9) discharging a firearm in a public place other than a public road or a shooting range
(10) displaying a firearm or other deadly weapon in a public place in a manner calculated to alarm
(11) discharging a firearm on or across a public road
(12) exposing one's anus or genitals in a public place being reckless about offending or alarming another person.

The mens rea of disorderly conduct is intentionally or knowingly engaging in one of the behaviors identified by the statute. All the acts constitute Class C misdemeanors, except for discharging a firearm in a public place and displaying a firearm or deadly weapon in a public place. They are punished as Class B misdemeanors.

Defenses to Prosecution

Section 42.04 provides an important defense to prosecution under 42.01(a)(5) - creating unreasonable noise. The same defense is available for prosecution under section 42.03 - obstructing a highway or other passageway. The defense provides that if conduct that would otherwise violate one of these statutes consists of speech or communication or gatherings to listen to speech or communication for the purpose of social protest, authorities must order defendants to move prior to arresting them if they have not yet harmed someone else's interests. If no such order was given or if the order was unreasonable, defendants must be exonerated.

Joe Blanco was convicted of disorderly conduct for intentionally making unreasonable noise in a public place. He had positioned the stereo speakers on his apartment porch so the sound of his music was directed toward the swimming pool area of the apartment complex. He had refused requests to turn down the stereo volume from his neighbors, the apartment management, and a police officer. He was arrested under section 42.01(a)(5) of the Penal Code. Blanco challenged the provision of the statute as overbroad and vague. In *Blanco v. State*, 761 S.W.2d 38 (Tex. App. - Houston [14th Dist.] 1988), the Court of Appeals affirmed his conviction by noting that the State's police powers include the right to protect the tranquility, quiet enjoyment, and well-being of a community. That only limit on that power is an individual constitutional right, such as the First Amendment right to free speech. In his case, the court concluded that the statute did not infringe on the right to free speech because section 42.04 restricts the reach of the unreasonable noise provision when constitutionally protected speech is involved and sufficiently protects an individual's rights. The court found that Blanco's conduct clearly fell within the proscribed activity, and he failed to show that the statute was unconstitutional as applied to him.

In *State v. Rivenburgh*, 933 S.W.2d 698 (Tex. App. - San Antonio 1996), the court reviewed a conviction for driving while intoxicated which started as a stop for the crime of disorderly conduct. The arresting officer testified that Rivenburgh was stopped at a red light, and when the light turned green, other motorists honked their horns because she was holding up traffic. The officer observed Rivenburgh make a vulgar gesture with her middle finger and mouth an obscenity in her rear view mirror. In his experience as a police officer, he testified that such gestures often cause fights so he proceeded to stop her for disorderly conduct. The court had to clarify whether the officer had the right to arrest Rivenburgh without a warrant for disorderly conduct in order to establish the legality of her arrest for driving while intoxicated.

Section 42.01 (a)(2) provides that a person can be arrested for disorderly conduct if he or she intentionally makes an offensive gesture in a public place which tends to incite an immediate breach of the peace. According to Texas courts, the offensive gesture or display must amount to fighting words that plainly tend to excite people to breach the peace. Harsh and insulting language does not generally rise to the fighting words level. Whether a particular gesture amounts to fighting words is a question of fact. The Court of Appeals upheld the trial judge's decision that Rivenburgh's gesture and the obscenity she mouthed were fighting words.

In *Nixon v. State*, 928 S.W.2d 212 (Tex. App. - Beaumont 1996), the issue was whether a person's backyard could be considered a public place under the disorderly conduct statute. Nixon was arrested in the backyard of his private residence for disorderly conduct. Cocaine was found on his person during a search incident to that arrest. He challenged the right of the police to arrest him for disorderly conduct on his own property, hoping to establish that his arrest was unlawful, and, therefore, so was the search. The court concluded that a residential backyard was a public place because a crowd of 50 or so persons gathered when the defendant became loud and abusive toward the police officer. A place is or is not public according to the facts and circumstances of a particular case.

> **Exercise:**
> As is evident in the *Rivenburgh* and *Nixon* cases, law enforcement often uses the right to arrest a person for disorderly conduct as a means to investigate more serious offenses. Find other cases where the police used a disorderly conduct charge as a way to investigate suspicions that more serious criminal activity was a foot. Is this an appropriate use of the statute? It is legal, but can discretion be abused? What advantages are there for police in having authority to use a crime like disorderly conduct to dig deeper into the facts of a suspicious situation?

RIOTING, OBSTRUCTING, AND DISTURBING

A riot is defined in section 42.02 as an assemblage of seven or more people engaged in conduct that:

(1) creates an immediate danger of damage to property or injury to persons
(2) substantially obstructs law enforcement or other governmental functions or services
(3) by force, threat of force, or physical action deprives a person of a legal right or disturbs any person's enjoyment of a legal right

The State must plead and prove that a defendant performed one of the enumerated acts. It is a defense to prosecution that the assemblage started lawfully and when one of the participants expressed intent to engage in riotous conduct, the defendant left the assembly. It is not a defense to prosecution that a person who was a part of the riot was acquitted, not arrested, prosecuted or convicted, was convicted of another offense, or was immune to prosecution.

The courts have ruled that the riot statute does not violate the First Amendment because it does not proscribe participation in a lawful assembly. By requiring knowing participation, the State must show the defendant participated knowing the assembly was resulting in unlawful activity. Mere presence at the scene of a riot does not make a person a party to a riot.

Section 42.03 prohibits obstructing highways or other passageways. It can be committed intentionally, knowingly, or recklessly. The actus reus includes obstructing streets, sidewalks, railways, waterways, elevators, aisles, hallways, entrances, or exits to which the public has access. It does not matter how the obstruction was created or whether the defendant was acting alone or with others. Passage must be blocked in such a way as to render it unreasonably inconvenient or hazardous. Merely slowing down passage or momentarily impeding passage does not violate the statute. The defendant's conviction was upheld because he refused to allow pedestrians to use the sidewalk and forced them to walk in mud on the street in *Haye v. State*, 634 S.W.2d 313 (Tex. Crim. App. 1982). The court affirmed the defendant's conviction for parking his truck across a ditch along the highway right-of-way and forcing a road crew to stop and leave their vehicle in *Brightbill v. State*, 734 S.W.2d 733 (Tex. App. - Amarillo 1987).

A second way to commit an offense under section 42.03 is to fail to obey a reasonable request or order to move by a peace officer, fireman, or person with the authority to control the premises. The State does not have to show that there was obstruction, it only needs to show that a defendant failed to obey an order designed to prevent obstruction.

Edna Louise Lauderback was convicted of obstructing a highway or other passageway after she had a disagreement with Olney Savings in Gainesville, Texas. She picketed the bank on foot for approximately five weeks. She then borrowed a wheel chair, attached a sign to it that stated "Olney Savings cripples women" and placed the wheelchair in a lane of traffic on a street in front of the bank. The street was busy and narrow with no parking available on it. The police received angry telephone calls from citizens who complained that the sign and chair obstructed the street. Lauderback refused a police officer's requests to move. She argued that public highways are open to everyone and where there are no sidewalks, a pedestrian can use the roadway. There was conflicting evidence as to whether Lauderback was handicapped. The court, however, affirmed her conviction, handicapped or not. The evidence showed that appellant obstructed a highway. It was not necessary that she actually cause a hazard. It was reasonable for police to ask her to move based on a potential hazard or the inconvenience she caused motorists. The court concluded that the statute did not abridge Lauderback's right to free speech because she could have picketed on the sides of the bank or on its parking lot.

Section 42.05 of the code proscribes intentionally preventing or disrupting a lawful meeting, procession, or gathering through physical actions or verbal utterances. An interesting case interpreting this section 42.05 Gardell Morehead who was convicted of disrupting a lawful meeting in *Morehead v. State*, 807 S.W.2d 577 (Tex. Crim. App. 1991). Gardell attended a national conference of a sorority at the Dallas Convention Center where civil rights leader Jesse Jackson was the speaker. Halfway through Rev. Jackson's speech, Morehead rose from his seat and began walking down the center aisle of the auditorium toward the podium. He yelled loudly that Jackson was a liar. Morehead continued yelling and interrupted Jackson's speech. Morehead was arrested after refusing an officer's request to leave.

The issue again was whether the Texas statute violated appellant's right to free speech. The Court of Criminal Appeals overturned Gardell's conviction because the jury was not properly instructed on the limits of section 42.05. The statute should be construed to criminalize only physical acts or verbal utterances that substantially impair the ordinary conduct of lawful meetings and thereby curtail the exercise of other people's First Amendment rights. The jury was not informed about the limits of the statute. The court's concern was that section 42.05 not be constructed too narrowly so as to criminalize all disturbances to lawful meetings. Some impairment of meetings is the price we pay to maintain the freedom of political expression under the Constitution. Individuals and groups who propose change sometimes engage in aggressive conduct. Some of that conduct must be considered constitutionally protected speech.

> **Exercises:**
> Other sections of Chapter 42 address the offense of initiating or communicating a false alarm, silent or abusive calls to 9-1-1, harassment by telephone or written communication, stalking, abuse of corpse, cruelty to animals, dog fighting, and discharge of a firearm. Read these sections and determine how law enforcement agencies, including which agencies, enforce these criminal activities.
>
> Refer to your local city or county ordinances and read those sections that address many of the same or similar offenses defined in Chapter 42. For example, Chapter 23 section 8 of the Fort Worth Municipal Code declares that any unreasonably loud, disturbing, unnecessary noise that causes material distress, discomfort, or injury to people with ordinary sensibilities is a nuisance and prohibited. The ordinance then goes on to specifically prohibit playing the radio, phonograph, or a musical instrument in such a manner between 10 p.m. and 7 a.m. And watch out for loud animals and birds that cause frequent or long-continuing noise!
>
> City ordinances also address conduct that is not addressed by state law. Houston City Ordinance Chapter 28 section 46 prohibits aggressive panhandling. The ordinance, which defines a panhandler as a solicitor and the person they are panhandling from the solicitee, provides:
>
>> Immediately upon any request from a solicitee to a solicitor, a solicitor who is in a public place (that is a street, sidewalk or other place that is open to the public) at the moment the request is made shall discontinue the solicitation until there is a space of at least eight feet between the solicitor and the solicitee or, in the alternative, discontinue all efforts to engage in the solicitation if within eight feet proximity to a requesting solicitee.
>
> The San Antonio Municipal Code, Chapter 21 section 7, makes it illegal to climb pecan trees in any public park or street within the city or to throw sticks, stones, or other missiles in order to gather pecans. Common city code ordinances prohibit such relatively innocuous behavior nowadays as spitting in public places.
>
> Check your city's code. Notice that although there is a lot of overlap, city codes cover a lot of circumstances not covered by state statute.
>
> Check your city code with respect to regulating sexually oriented businesses: where they can be located, hours of operation, advertising, licensing, restrictions on how dancers can dress and act toward customers. These regulations have been especially controversial in large cities where such businesses generate large profits.

OTHER PUBLIC ORDER OFFENSES

Public intoxication is an offense defined by section 49.02 of the Penal Code. The crime is committed when a person appears in a public place while intoxicated to the degree that he or she might endanger themselves or another. The danger does not have to be immediate and the arresting officer does not have to specify an identifiable danger. In *Bentley v. State*, 535 S.W.2d 651 (Tex. Crim. App. 1976), the court found it sufficient that in the officer's opinion the defendant would have attempted to drive an automobile were he not arrested. It is a defense to prosecution if the alcohol or substance was administered for therapeutic purposes and as part of treatment by a licensed physician.

Chapter 43 provides for two sets of crimes involving public indecency. The first set addresses prostitution, promoting prostitution, and compelling prostitution. The second set addresses obscenity: its definition, obscene display or distribution, promoting obscenity, the sale, distribution or display of harmful material to a minor, sexual performance by a child, possession or promotion of child pornography. Some of these offenses are also addressed in city ordinances.

Chapter 46 addresses weapons offenses including unlawful possession of a firearm, prohibited weapons, places where weapons are prohibited, hoax bombs, penalty for an offense committed in a weapon-free zone, and making a firearm accessible to a child.

Illegal gambling is defined in the Chapter 47 offenses. In addition to defining public intoxication, Chapter 49 defines the driving while intoxicated offenses and intoxication manslaughter.

FINAL COMMENTS ON CRIMES AGAINST PUBLIC ORDER AND MORALS

This chapter focused on crimes against public order. Although they can involve less serious criminal behavior, these offenses raise interesting issues. Authorities often use crimes like disorderly conduct as pretexts to investigate more serious criminal conduct. There are frequent allegations from many communities that public order statutes are used to harass citizens rather than to keep peace. Some public order crimes raise First Amendment free speech issues. It is easy to dismiss public order crimes as minor. As the first line of offenses imposing criminal sanctions, however, public order statutes affect large numbers of people and leave lasting impressions about the workings of law enforcement agencies and the courts. Out of necessity, they are broadly written and give police wide discretionary powers.

MULTIPLE CHOICE QUESTIONS

1. The disorderly conduct statute in Texas makes it illegal to carry a weapon in a public place even if it is carefully placed in an appropriate carrying case and not being waived or brandished to the public.

    a. True
    b. False

2. A person who unwittingly gets caught up in a riot, not intending, wanting, or knowing that what started as a peaceful assembly is now disturbing another person's legal rights is not guilty of the crime of riot.

    a. True
    b. False

3. It is not illegal to use indecent or profane language in public as long as the language does not tend to incite an immediate breach of the peace.

    a. True
    b. False

4. A tomahawk is considered a club that can be carried illegally under certain circumstances.

    a. True
    b. False

5. It is not necessary that authorities order persons who are engaging in unreasonable noise to stop before they can arrest the offender.

    a. True
    b. False

ANSWER KEY

CHAPTER ONE	CHAPTER TWO	CHAPTER THREE	CHAPTER FOUR	CHAPTER FIVE	CHAPTER SIX	CHAPTER SEVEN
1. c	1. b	1. b	1. a	1. b	1. b	1. d
2. d	2. b	2. c	2. c	2. c	2. c	2. c
3. c	3. c	3. c	3. a	3. a	3. c	3. c
4. d	4. d	4. b	4. a	4. b	4. a	4. a
5. c	5. a	5. c	5. a	5. b	5. b	5. b
6. b	6. d	6. c	6. b	6. c	6. b	6. c
7. d	7. b	7. c	7. d	7. b	7. b	7. b
8. a	8. b	8. b	8. b	8. b	8. b	8. b
9. d	9. a	9. b	9. c	9. b	9. b	9. a
10. d	10. c			10. c	10. c	10. c
11. a						
12. c						
13. a						
14. b						
15. b						

CHAPTER EIGHT	CHAPTER NINE	CHAPTER TEN	CHAPTER ELEVEN	CHAPTER TWELVE	CHAPTER THIRTEEN
1. c	1. b	1. d	1. c	1. b	1. b
2. d	2. b	2. b	2. b	2. b	2. a
3. a	3. b	3. b	3. d	3. c	3. a
4. b	4. b	4. a	4. a	4. d	4. a
5. c	5. c	5. b	5. a	5. d	5. b
6. b	6. a	6. c	6. c	6. a	
7. b	7. b	7. a	7. c	7. b	
8. c	8. c	8. d	8. b	8. b	
9. b	9. b	9. b	9. c	9. b	
10. b	10. a	10. c	10. c	10. a	
		11. b			
		12. d			
		13. b			
		14. b			
		15. b			